LEARNING IN SPITE OF LABELS

Practical Teaching Tips And
A Christian Perspective Of Education

Information in this book should not be construed as
or take the place of professional counsel
or legal advice.

Written and Illustrated by
Joyce Herzog

Forward by
Sharon Grimes

First Printing, April 1994
Second Printing, April 1995
Third Printing, August 1997

ISBN 1-882514-13-0
Printed in the USA

Internet: www.greenleafpress.com
3761 Highway 109 N., Unit D
Lebanon, TN 37087
615-449-1617

GREENLEAF
P · R · E · S · S

OTHER WORKS BY AUTHOR
Joyce Herzog

(see order form on pages 223)

The Scaredy Cat Reading System

(Phonics that have worked where others have failed)

- The Story of LetterMaster
- Level 1 – PreReading Kit
- Level 2 – Beginner's Book
- Level 3 – Advanced Beginner's Book
- Level 4 – Rules...and Fun!

History in His Hands

(Read Aloud and Study Guides)

- Volume One – Ancient History
- Volume Two – Early Christian History and Middle Ages

Stepping Stones to Bigger Faith for Little People

(A Family Devotion)

Luke's List

(Checklist of virtually all wisdom, knowledge and skills that a *mature adult should know.*)

Luke's List Academics

(Nearly all academic from kindergarten through eighth grade.

DEDICATION

*For Mom, who would have worked with me
on this if Alzheimers hadn't destroyed her mind
and body long before her time.*

For Elizabeth, Tim, Robert, and Edward...

For Amy, Marcia, Joel, Bobby, Tina, Patty, and Melissa...

For Scott, Michael, Ryan, and Paula...

*For Amy and Ann,
Billy and Steven,
and Shaun and Adrianne,
the twins...*

For David, Jon, Bryan, Jonathan, Tom, and James...

For Elizabeth, Eric, Joseph, and Rebecca...

*and all the ones whose faces I still see,
but whose names are somewhere in the distant foggy past...
who taught me when I thought I was teaching them.*

CONTENTS

CONTENTS (CONTINUED)

SECTION FOUR: And Furthermore

ACKNOWLEDGEMENTS

Many thanks and prayers of blessing and heavenly reward:

to my husband Tom for putting up with me through the writing of this, for all his encouragement as it came to be, and for the nights he lost sleep fixing the computer, proofreading the copy, and compiling the index which almost wasn't.

to Diana Waring whose humorous storytelling, singing, and love of people who lived before our time inspired me to include the mini-biographies.

to Elizabeth Farewell for inspiring the chapter on *Teeny Tiny Teaching Tips* with her idea about table settings.

to Tina Farewell who tells me the truth even when I don't want to hear it and prays for me when nothing else works.

to Virginia Hein, and her 100-year-old mother, who are always there to listen and encourage us in our many projects.

to Jeanette Macaluso, Cathy Duffy, Margie Callaghan, and Sharon Grimes, who lovingly proofread and commented on the organization of this book in time for me to respond **before** it went to the printer.

to Sharon Grimes who gives me moral support, teaches me many things I should have known already, and kindly consented to writing the foreword for this book.

and to Bernie Cinkoske and Rob and Cyndy Shearer who believed in me and this work enough to put their money behind it.

FOREWORD

Welcome, fellow travelers. I, too, have been on a long journey in search of answers for my disabled child. Our paths up to this point have been varied, but I know that if you are reading this, you, too, probably have or know a child with a disability.

I don't know if that child is one with a physical or mental impairment, or both, but I do know that disabilities vary greatly from child to child. Many challenged children are struggling with learning disabilities, and their parents share that struggle. "Something just isn't right with my child!"

As I look back over the many miles our family's journey with Hannah has already covered, it is a blessing to also see that every time we cried out to God for answers, He answered. Oh, it wasn't always according to *our* schedule, and it wasn't always the answer *we* were looking for, but God has revealed His sovereignty again and again, and we rejoice!

One of the "answers" has been Joyce Herzog. The Lord brought us together for a "divine" appointment in June of 1993 in a place that was far from both of our homes. As I spent a weekend with Joyce and learned from her, my heart was blessed with her gentle spirit and gift of helps. Her lifework reflects the compassion she feels for parents of learning disabled children. She affirms to each mother that the most important degree is not an M.A., but a M.A.M.A. as we advocate as no one else can for our "special needs" children.

I encourage those of you who have concerns about your child to start getting the help that you need. This book is a good starting point! Utilize the resource suggestions; keep accurate records of your observations and your child's development; ask lots of questions; and remember to be open and honest as you continue your journey.

No one knows better than I the tremendous amount of emotional energy that is required to walk this path, but God's promise in Isaiah 40:31 remains true: "They that wait upon the Lord shall renew their strength; they shall mount up with wings as eagles; they shall run and not be weary; they shall walk, and not faint."

Don't faint, dear friend - walk with God, take good care of yourself, learn all that you can, and determine to do whatever God wants you to do to help your very special child "grow in wisdom and stature, and in favor with God and man." Don't ever forget that God has a very special plan for your child, and that, by His grace, and with Joyce's helpful advice in this book, your child *can* LEARN in spite of LABELS!

May God bless you as you continue on your journey.

Sharon   Grimes
Founder New York State Loving Education at Home (LEAH)

Sharon Grimes

PREFACE

The spring before I began to write this book, five different speakers on the subject of learning disabilities defined many words and discussed much theory. They gave many interpretations of the law but gave little practical information and few teaching techniques that might work with these unique children. This book is to help you meet the needs of children who struggle with learning. It may appear on the surface that they are failing to learn. In reality, they are learning to fail! Failure-oriented is the term I came up with many years ago. Don't kid yourself into believing that these children sit, unsuccessful, in the classrooms of our country learning nothing at all. Everyone learns something every day. They may learn to expect failure. They may learn to stop trying. They may learn to find success in getting into trouble. One thing is sure. They are learning!

I have been a learning disabilities teacher for more than twenty-five years. At the time I started working the field was brand new. There were neither experts nor answers. There was no one to go to, no curriculum that worked for me, no help to be found. So I scrounged, adapted, and created. I tried new techniques, new approaches, new materials, and new ways of thinking about these children. Over the years, the system changed labels, recommendations, and regulations. Gradually "experts" appeared who had studied statistics and books and someone else's studies. All the while, I kept plugging away day after day and year after year. I found things that worked with some of the children and a few things that seemed to benefit all the children. My goal in this book is to increase your success through these proven insights and techniques.

I am a Christian. I believe that all our actions affect our relationship with God. If we choose to act according to His Word and His Way, we please Him. If we choose to go our own way, we will struggle with everything and everyone.

Throughout the book I refer to the children with learning disabilities in the masculine gender. Most of the children I worked with over the years were boys, so when I refer to them as a group I think of them as boys. In the first years over ninety per cent of the children I worked with were boys. You will notice also that most of the illustrations are boys. I seem to have a natural affinity for drawing them. A few illustrations come from my collection of antique schoolbooks. They were produced in the 1890's. They have a sweet flavor I was unable to capture.

It is interesting that by the last year I taught the class was almost evenly divided between boys and girls. As I pondered this I could come up with only one thing that had changed. Children were now being herded into formal group learning situations at younger and younger ages. Most boys develop readiness for academic learning later than girls. When I began teaching, formal education began at age five and many boys were not developmentally ready for formal learning or for intense visual and visual motor work. Twenty-five years later, most children are now in a day-care situation where reading and writing are started with three and four-year-olds. A few are ready. Many are not, especially among the boys. As the age for formal education dropped, more and more girls were identified as "learning disabled."

About the term learning disabled: I don't like it either. Challenged is more appropriate, but whatever term you use, it fits us all! I am disabled when it comes to trying to understand what my husband says about how something works. I don't even care. I just want it to work! He is disabled when it comes to finding things and understanding spatial concepts. Let's face it, we are all disabled!

The system, in order to provide additional services, puts labels on many children. They may be identified as learning disabled, mentally retarded, autistic, emotionally disturbed, slow learner, ADD and on and on. But the system is not the only one to label. Parents do it all the time. "She's the smart one." "He's just lazy." "What's *wrong* with you?"

I believe we have created the problems faced by many learning disabled children by forcing them into structured, fine-motor, and close-up vision tasks which involve symbols and abstract concepts before they are developmentally ready. This is further complicated by the tension and pressure to succeed and the frustration and failure experienced by the many children who truly try to do what they are not yet capable of doing.

At times we all find ourselves bent beneath a load that seems too much to bear. We have more questions than answers...more problems than successes. Realize the children with learning difficulties feel that way most of the time. They notice others who understand much faster and verbalize their responses more clearly. Others get more praise and approval from the adults in their lives. And they don't understand. They know only that they want desperately to be like their more successful friends, but don't know how.

No matter what labels have been put on your child, he was created to learn. Let's concentrate on our ables, not our labels!

Let's explore some ways to help!

INTRODUCTION:
TEACHING OR LEARNING?

Look for a moment at the difference between teaching and learning. True teaching is facilitating learning, but often:

Teaching is presenting information. Teachers lecture. Teachers talk. Teachers assign reading. Teachers give tests. Teachers grade tests (which tell more about what and how the teacher has taught than what the children have learned). As soon as a teacher has presented the material he usually moves immediately on to new material with little regard to how many children have mastered the material or how well they know it.

Learning is different. Let's think of potty training. If you are reading this, you have probably gotten beyond that stage with your children. When you were potty training what was your goal? Did you expect 80% of your children to recite the proper steps of correct pottying? Did you stop when half your children could get a grade of A when asked what was the first step of using the toilet? Of course not! You continued until every child could do what they were supposed to!

Did they all learn in a group? At the same age? Of course not! Did you label any of them potty retarded, potty disabled, or potty impaired? Certainly not, unless the physician found a legitimate reason why they were unable to learn this skill at this time. And then what did you do? Go on to other skills and forever leave your ten year old in diapers? No, you continued working until it was proven by behavior that the concept had been learned!

If we have twins, or more, do we wait until all are ready for the lesson and then group them in the potty and give a lecture on "The Steps to Potty Training?" Do we follow that lecture by oral drill or written assignments on the steps in potty training in order to determine which of them really got it? And if one has mastered the skill, do we keep him sitting on the potty till the others catch up? Or let him start training the next child? Of course not! We praise and encourage and instruct each one individually.

When we potty train a child, we take them one at a time and work with them and encourage them and reward them until **they are successfully completing the desired action on their own without adult supervision or prompting!**

We teach until they have learned!

We continue whether this takes weeks, months or years. We never give up trying. We may lessen the emphasis, alter the tactics, even back off for a time; but we never give up until the child is successfully completing the desired action on his own without adult supervision or prompting!

It is time to stop teaching subjects!

It is time to begin teaching children!

All children can learn! A diagnosis of learning disability, ADD (Attention Deficit Disorder), ADHD (Attention Deficit Hyperactive Disorder), autism, or mental retardation does not mean that the child can not learn. It means that the teacher will be more than ever responsible to adapt and individualize the instruction and the demands. It means that the teacher must be ready to define steps to success, redefine goals, concentrate on the ten percent which is **really** important, and listen to the silent messages of the child!

All children can learn!

Let's explore some ways
to assist your child in this process!

SECTION ONE

WHAT DO I NEED TO KNOW?

What Does It Feel Like To Be Learning Disabled?

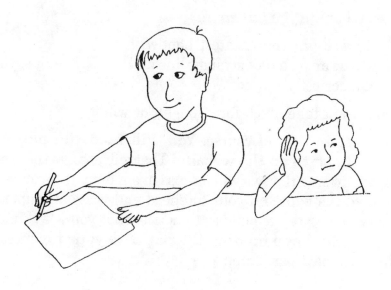

T he first thing you need to know is what it is like to have a learning disability. The following activity will give you the rare opportunity to experience what it feels like to be learning disabled. You will need a piece of paper which is not attached to a notebook and a pen or pencil. I will ask you to do a very simple thing.

I will tell you what to do, **but before you do it, I will add one other teeny little instruction,** so get ready, but do not actually do it until I give the final instruction and tell you to do it.

You are going to write down a date that is important to you: such as the date of your birth, your marriage, or the birth of your child. You will use the numeral way of writing dates. The second thing you are to write is the name of the city and state where that dated thing happened. If you write the date of your marriage, you will also write the name of the city and state where you were married.

That sounds simple enough, doesn't it?

4 - 25 - 59

As you write, notice your thought process. What are you *thinking*?

Try to write in your neatest handwriting. Try to write on a nice straight line with the letters perfectly spaced.

San Diego, California

That won't take much forethought, or will it?

There is a catch, of course. **You will hold the paper on your forehead to do the writing!** That will change the task in an important way that we will discuss in a moment. For now, you are to hold the paper on your forehead and write an important date, city and state. Remember to notice what you are thinking! After you write, **keep holding the paper to your forehead** as you read the next paragraph.

Do not take it down and look at it just yet!

Write now, but don't take the paper down until you read the next paragraph!

Did you have to think about the direction to move your pen? Did you forget which letter or number came next? Was it more difficult than usual? Did you do your best?

Take the paper down now and look at your work. Did you reverse any letters or numbers? Did you write the whole thing in mirror writing? How was your letter formation and spacing? What grade would you get if I graded your paper for handwriting with a group of papers where the students were allowed to write normally? How would you feel if I judged you on the basis of this paper? How would you feel if everyone else in the room could write normally and you had to continue writing this way for the rest of the year, but were graded on the same norms as everyone else?

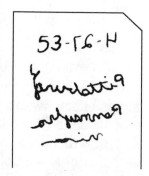

How would you feel if you could only make improvements by looking in a mirror and **never** could take the paper down?

Many people reverse letters and write poorly. Many very good writers with exceptional writing ability will find that their paper resembles that of a young learning disabled child! Why? What changed? Your learning ability? No. Your skill level? No. The **only** change was the orientation of the paper in relation to your body!

One small change with major effect!

But isn't that what we do to children when they enter school?

Children are learners from birth.

Yet most children with learning disabilities are not recognized in those first five years. They learn to eat and talk and dress themselves. They learn to tie shoes, ride bikes, listen to a story, and stack blocks. Most of them learn in the normal sequence and on a very normal schedule.

Why?

Are their teachers carefully screened and advised on how to handle their unique problems? No. The problem is really another small change with a major effect. We bring a child to school, sit him down at a desk, and present him with symbols. At home a chair is a chair. No matter which direction it faces, it is still a chair. Yet now the orientation of a symbol changes its value! A 6 and a 9 are different only in their spatial orientation. The same is true with b, d, p, and q. Only the position in space changes, but these two numerals and four letters now have different names and different functions.

One small change with a major effect!

This is only one of the ways we change the child's environment when we send him to school. His teacher is no longer the person he has known since birth. The surroundings are no longer his own home and family. The materials he is familiar with are gone. His freedom is severely limited. We place time limits on his performance. We require for eight hours that he does what we ask, when we ask, in the manner we decide, and that he sits how and where we designate. The tasks we ask him to do are more abstract, more specific, and usually demand one right answer.

At home our learner took in information through play, trial and error, listening, and watching. As an infant his visual skills were limited, so he tasted, touched, banged, sat on, and threw to hear and experience a response. As his visual skills developed, he gradually gave up some of the tasting and touching. This development in children varies considerably. Some learn faster than others. Some have gone further than others. That was acceptable when they were home and not being compared to other children their own ages. Did you ever notice that in a family there are rarely two or more children the same age? They come naturally in stair steps! This is God's way to discourage direct comparisons.

Now they have arrived at school age and suddenly we expect them all to be ready for the same information given in the same manner at the same rate.

And we wonder why some don't experience success.

We should rather wonder that the vast majority DO experience success!

Notes...

CHAPTER
TWO

A LOOK
AT LEARNING

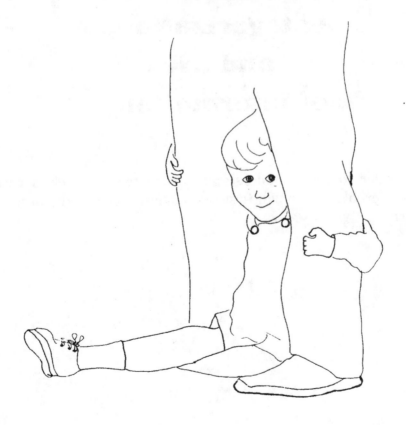

Learning is a lifetime activity of normal people.

Learning begins very early in life.

Learning should never end.

What is learning?

Learning is the assimilation, categorization, and use of information.

In order to better understand how to teach the child with learning problems, we will first take a closer look at the process of learning.

LEARNING TAKES PLACE IN THREE STAGES:

| 1. | **Receiving Information** |

| 2. | **Processing Information** |

| 3. | **Expressing Information** |

Let's take a closer look at each of the three stages of learning:

Step One: Receiving Information

Receiving information begins
even before birth!

Information is received through the senses:

tasting with the mouth,

touching with fingers and hands,

smelling with the nose,

hearing with the ears,

seeing with the eyes.

13

God has given these senses to us to receive information about the physical world in which we live.

Some of us are more skilled than others in each of these senses. Some of us have developed our senses better than others. Some develop skill automatically, others need specific training in seeing and hearing effectively. This may be an area where you notice that your children differ considerably. One may seem to take naturally to coloring, drawing, writing, puzzles and other close vision activities. Another child may seem to run, not walk, involve themselves only in large muscle activities, and rarely pick up a book or a pencil.

If your child prefers large muscle activities, there may be no problem. But if he refuses most small motor activities, you may need to look into a need for visual skills development. Have him copy a simple pattern with blocks, trace a design with his fingers, catch and throw a ball. Encourage coloring, drawing, and painting with fingers or large brushes. Some children need specific

training to develop the visual skills needed for close up work! If your child continues to avoid close up tasks (except tv or video games) consider the possibility of a need for visual training. See Chapter 17.

When we work with small children, we usually still give them the opportunity to touch and handle, to move and explore.

14

Within a year or two, we limit those experiences or eliminate them and expect the child to sit in a seat, look from a distance, listen constantly, and write his response. And most of his visual input is now in symbols which he may or may not have the skill to handle. If we find he is suddenly rebellious and resistant, there may be a reason! We may have changed the environment before he had the skills to adjust!

If your child does not seem to respond to auditory stimulus, have his hearing checked. If there is no problem, begin to develop his listening skill. Do this through reading aloud picture books. Stop frequently to reinforce what you say through the pictures. Teach him to recite short rhymes. Have him follow verbal directions (given one at a time at first). Involve him in listening for the doorbell, telephone, stove timer, etc. See Chapter 18 for more information.

Since the auditory and visual skills are most important for "school" tasks, concentrate on developing these primary skills before you expect him to use them as an avenue to learning!

Step Two: Processing Information

Once the learner has received the information, what is next? The information disappears inside this thing called a brain which **processes the information**. There are many theories out there about brain development, division of labor and skills, and training brain processes. I will not be dealing with any of these as it is not possible to open the brain and assess what is happening.

We can only evaluate information processing through observing the last step of learning.

We'll get to that in a moment.

Processing information

involves three steps:

The information must be

stored,

remembered,

and

retrieved.

Storing information — involves categorizing and classifying, or relating the new information to what is already known. If information is given without relating it to the known, the learner will categorize it himself, but his categories are based on little information and therefore tend to be quite faulty. The learning process is greatly enhanced if the teacher starts with something that is known and moves step by step through comparisons to the unknown. This process is further enhanced if these steps are easy to picture in the mind.

Remembering the information — may involve short term memory which is seconds to minutes or long term which is days to years. The two memory types are separate and someone who is excellent at one may be extremely weak in the other. My husband is a prime example. Tom's long term memory is one of the best I've ever seen. He remembers more bits of information than seems possible. Yet he is continually frustrated by a weak short-term memory which cannot recall where he set something down a few seconds ago.

Memory is enhanced by increasing the number of senses involved. If the information can be heard, recited and pictured, it is more likely to be retained. Setting ideas to music or gentle rhythms further increases the likelihood that they will be remembered. Use caution here, though. This can be overdone. If the songs are too similar or concentrate too much on rhythm they may complicate rather than assist learning.

Retrieving the information — means pulling it back later to express it, use it, or relate it to new information. Retrieving information depends on three things:

1. **How and how well the information was learned.** Information which was barely understood and never applied to different situations will not be remembered long. Head knowledge is soon forgotten. What the heart and hands learn are long remembered.

2. **Whether the information was related to anything which was previously known.** Isolated bits of information are less likely to be retained. Information which is woven into many relationships is more easily recalled.

3. **How relevant the *learner* considered the information at the time it was presented.** We may present information which we consider crucial and expect that the learner will automatically agree. Most learners categorize information quickly: important, remember this; or unimportant, don't bother to remember.

How can we evaluate an individual's ability to receive and process information? We cannot open the skull and look. These first two steps of learning go on behind closed doors within the brain and can only be evaluated by the **third step of learning: expression**.

Step Three: Expressing Information

There are several ways of expressing information: say, do, write, point, dance, draw, make or move something.

Let's think about our toddler again. He expresses what he knows primarily by showing you that he can **do** something. If you want to know whether he learned to tie his shoe, do you ask him to recite the steps in the process of shoe tying? If you want to know whether he is potty trained, do you want a recitation similar to this: "When I feel the urge, I will walk to the bathroom, turn on the light, close the door, walk...?" Of course not! We evaluate whether he has learned by whether he **does** the right thing at the right time.

What happens when we take the learner to "school"? We change the means of expression. There are too many children to have each child do something. There are too many children to have each one say something. So we teach them to listen, read, and write. Then they spend the remainder of their school years listening and reading and writing! Why?

18

Because it is beneficial for the learner? No, because it is easier for us to evaluate!

Of the many ways to express information, the most common means of expression used in school are speaking and writing. Because of the number of learners and time limitations, speaking is often limited. Because it takes more time for the teacher to read long answers, writing is often limited to circling the answer; choosing A, B, or C; or underlining information.

With our toddler, we welcomed pointing, demonstrating, making, doing. When he entered school we limited the means of expression. Some children are deprived of the opportunity to learn to the limit of their potential by these restrictions **we have forced on them!** If they are not good at writing, or following a line of circles and numbers, or don't excel at precision, they fail. And even those who learn to succeed in the system may also learn that it is profitable not to think, not to offer alternatives, and not to challenge the status quo.

We will look at some alternative ways to express information in a future chapter.

Notes...

Chapter
Three

Behavior
and Strengths

B asically a child with learning disabilities is one who, in spite of a normal or high IQ and adequate effort and learning opportunity, has not achieved up to expectations in one or more areas of academic achievement.

Behavioral Characteristics

There are behavior similarities which are characteristic of children with learning disabilities. This is not to say that any one child will have all of these behavior characteristics, or that children who are not learning disabled will have none of these characteristics. It means that a child who is learning disabled will have these characteristics with more frequency and intensity.

Behavior characteristics common to the learning disabled:

1. **Impulsive:** These children do not seem to predict the consequences of their decisions or behavior. They seem totally unaware, before or after, that their actions have created a situation.

2. **Hyperactive or hypoactive:** Hyperactive children seldom stop moving. Their brain and body seem to be in constant motion. Hypoactive children move little. They seem distant and uninterested.

3. **Inattentive and short attention span:** These children have difficulty focusing on anything and do not look you in the eye. They may seem to be in their own little world.

4. **Easily distracted:** These children pay attention to everything and do not differentiate between important and unimportant stimulus.

5. **Hard to motivate:** It is especially hard to motivate these children to do what you want them to do. They are too busy doing nothing or doing what they choose.

6. **Easily Frustrated:** These children have little tolerance for struggling. Often all of life is a struggle and they can't take on one more challenge.

7. **Selective memory (short or long term, visual or auditory):** It is easy to think that these children remember only what they want to, for they can truly remember only what they consider really important, if they remember anything at all.

8. **Difficulty following directions:** They can seldom keep their minds focused on a task long enough to complete it. If the instructions are involved they may not remember them.

9. **Variable performance from day to day:** You are convinced they understand or have mastered a skill only to have them act like they never heard the concept the next time you mention it.

10. **Poor coordination:** They may trip over nothing, drop everything, and be very poor at sports. They may have difficulty controlling fine muscles and do poorly at tasks like writing, coloring in the lines, and moving a game piece.

11. **May get "lost" in space or time:** They may not remember where they are, where they are headed, or what time of day it is. This is especially noticeable as they get into junior or senior high and cannot keep on a schedule.

12. **Frequently responds inappropriately:** These children may laugh when in sad or frightening situations and cry or throw a temper tantrum at a party.

13. **Overreacts to change:** They may be rigid in schedule demands or need warning before a change of activity.

14. **Has trouble turning off a behavior:** They may not seem to notice that an activity or conversation has moved on. They may need verbal and physical reminder to stop and switch gears.

15. **Misunderstands (or misuses) familiar concepts, words, people:** This is a hard to understand characteristic. These children may consistently call a spoon a scoop or not understand who "Aunt Joan" is even after many explanations.

16. **Uses language inappropriately or below developmental expectations:** May be saying "Me go." long after his peers are more articulate.

17. **Easily over-stimulated:** Since they over-react to everything, they may need to be kept away from places like circuses, busy playgrounds, or cafeterias until they demonstrate skill in controlling their emotions.

18. **Disorganization:** These children frequently forget important materials, lose their places, and have difficulty following sequences. They may not be able to get everything together to begin a task.

19. **Unrealistic Goal Setting:** These children are very poor at estimating the amount of time and energy needed to accomplish a task and are therefore very poor at setting realistic short-term and long-term goals.

Strengths

It has been my experience that these students also have some fine strengths.

1. Many of them know every advertising jingle they ever heard and **learn readily through music and rhythm.**

2. They are often **quite logical and precise**

3. They **know people and predict behavior** of friends and those in authority better than they predict the consequences of their own movements and decisions.

4. These children often **know "everything** there is to know" **about something they like.** They may have memorized what car every family drives to church or the batting averages of the pitchers of the New York Yankees.

5. **They seek meaning.** They do not want to be involved in activities unless they believe it has some meaning for their future. "Why do I have to do this?" is a frequent question.

6. Because these children have often suffered enormously as they mature **they have very tender and sympathetic feelings toward the underdog.**

7. Many of the children who have problems learning academics are **very artistic.**

8. These children are **often very creative** and if not forced to "do it my way" will come up with a more creative (and sometimes better) way of thinking about or accomplishing a task.

9. These children are **often very spiritually sensitive.** They seem to have a special hot line to heaven. If this is encouraged and fed, they are capable of accomplishing much in the kingdom of God!

Chapter Four

Issues to Consider

1. Scripture Guidelines

Proverbs 22:6 Train up a child in the way he should go: and when he is old, he will not depart from it.

Train him to the correct response, do not just tell him.

Up Lift him up, do not drag him down with impossibilities.

A Child He will need individual instruction.

In You cannot lead him where you have not been!

The Way One way, not alternative lifestyles.

He should Teach him right from wrong. He needs the truth.

Go Train him early to be involved, not to sit on the sidelines.

Psalms 145: 4, 10-12. One generation shall praise thy works to another, and shall declare thy mighty acts. All thy works shall praise thee, O Lord; and thy saints shall bless thee. They shall speak of the glory of thy kingdom, and talk of thy power; to make known to the sons of men his mighty acts, and the glorious majesty of his kingdom.

Our first responsibility must be to teach our children of the mighty works and glory of God's kingdom.

Proverbs 9:9. Give instruction to a wise man, and he will be yet wiser: teach a just man and he will increase in learning.

We are responsible to provide the opportunity for our children to learn wisdom and truth. He is learning from what he hears and sees and experiences. Make sure he hears, sees, and experiences truth.

Deuteronomy 2: 10. And there arose another generation after them, which knew not the Lord, nor yet the works which he had done for Israel.

We are never more than one generation away from extinction as Christians. These children will have a special need to be specifically taught principles and application. If you don't teach him these skills, who will?

Deuteronomy 6: 6 and 7. And these words, which I command thee this day, shall be in thine heart: And thou shalt teach them diligently unto thy children, and shalt talk of them when thou sittest in thine house, and when thou walkest by the way, when thou liest down, and when thou risest up.

The scriptures, the truth, must first be instilled in your own heart. Then teach them formally, sinking them into your children's hearts through word pictures and personal application. Then advertise them to the world. Speaking the truth to our children should be as natural and as frequent as breathing.

II Timothy 3: 16. All scripture is given by inspiration of God, and is profitable for doctrine, for reproof, for correction, for instruction in righteousness.

We don't have to look for magic curriculums or methods for teaching our children. We do need to surround and bathe them in the truth of the Scriptures and their application in daily decisions and events of life. To do this, we must ourselves be immersed in study and meditation on the truths we seek to instill in our children. We cannot teach what we have not learned! We cannot lead where we have not gone!

II Peter 1:3. His divine power has given us all things that pertain unto life and godliness.

Special needs children, too, have been given all things needed for life and godliness! They may be unable to meet some goals of man, but they are fully capable of meeting the goals of God!

2. What is a learning disability?

Simply put, a learning disability is a discrepancy between reality and a prediction. The prediction is based on evaluation of the past, the potential, and performance. These areas must be measured and compared to a norm:

Past Experience and Behavior including birth trauma, learning opportunities, and language experiences. Behavior characteristics may be as much related to a poor environment at home, a poor relationship to this year's teacher, an allergy, poorly developed visual and auditory skills, or stress which the child has internalized and may not even be able to identify.

Potential is determined by the administration of an intelligence (IQ) test, generally given by a school psychologist in an individual setting. This means that a relative or complete stranger spends an hour asking a child to answer questions or perform tasks in a quiet room. He then scores the test and uses that experience to make predictions regarding what that child is capable of learning in the best environment. Although IQ supposedly is related to ability and "potential," all it can really measure is the probable level of school success if the child continues to learn at the rate he has in the past as measured by a single performance. I have seen too many children with abuse or neglect or merely lack of opportunity whose IQs shot up ten or more points. The only change was some good teaching and exposure to the world of learning and information in a warm and accepting environment.

Performance combines teacher and parent observation with tested areas. I have seen a quickly administered test (fifteen minutes to evaluate a wide range of academic achievement) considered more important than years of classroom performance. Achievement reflects the teaching methods thus employed, the child's attitude toward learning, the type of test used, the child's health or mental attitude on the test day, and the child's test-taking ability.

3. Is there such a thing as learning disabilities?

After twenty-five years working in the field, I'd honestly have to say I don't know. Don't leave. Listen a moment...

Learning disabilities has been defined and therefore it exists. Yet diagnosis is merely a judgement call based on comparing one child with an "average" child on several issues.

Some people learn more easily than others. Some need more help in different ways and in different subjects. All people need help in some way learning something. Yet all people can learn given the proper environment for learning and the appropriate (for them) methods and materials. Once I had honed my skills as a teacher, I felt confident I could teach any student almost anything **if**:

- The student was cooperative.

- We had enough time.

- I was able to control the learning environment.

Am I a super-human person? No. I have experience, but the real secret is that God made people ready and able to learn. We have standardized an environment which is conducive to learning certain information and behaviors for some children and very frustrating for others. We have created some of our own problems by forcing children into boxes in which they cannot possibly fit.

Some problems which affect learning and can be detected and resolved are seldom considered. Because teachers are not generally qualified in these areas, they struggle with what they can control and ignore what they don't understand. Instead, a referral should be made for expert evaluation of some critical factors:

1. Allergies

2. Visual Skills

3. Auditory perception

31

I was continually frustrated by the children who almost fit and yet could get no help. The very bright child who needed help but was working too close to grade level (even though his potential was to be far above grade level) to get help. The child who scored too low on IQ to qualify for LD and too high on IQ to qualify for mentally retarded, so even if there were discrepancies enough to warrant LD profile, there was no help available.

All of life is a learning opportunity for every person! Don't push learning behind the walls of a school and make it the responsibility of a group of people who have no lifelong interest in the well-being of each student!

4. Education Versus School

School treats all the same,
gives all the same,
produces all the same.

Education is
preparing your child
to live out the
individual and personal
calling of God.

If you take school home, you might as well keep your children
in the system.

> If you don't educate your child,
> no matter where he goes to school,
> you will lose him to the world.

Education begins in the heart.
Education begins in the home.

5. What Is Really Important?

That your child:

Know the Bible
Build Character
Know God
Cover Subjects
Learn Basic Academics
Deal Constructively with Conflict
Be Prepared for Adult Living
Have at Least One Highly Developed Skill
Be "Educated"
Be Culturally Literate
Be a "Good Sport"
Be Good at Sports
Exhibit Normal Behavior
Have a Relationship with God
Have a Relationship with Family

Plan his education to develop the most important things first. Do not spend a lifetime teaching academics and neglect developing the spiritual nature of your child.

6. What Placement is Best?

Factors to Consider:

Home Education

- Do you have or can you cultivate a heart for learning?
- Are you willing and able to devote your heart and time to your child (children?) for this period of his life?
- Are you willing and able to devote your heart and time for this period of your life?

Public School

- What program is available?
- What teachers will he work with?
- Can he tolerate the needed interactions with other children?
- Will he learn anything besides avoidance behaviors and a tough spirit?

Private School

- What approach does it have?
- What is done with children who learn differently?
- Can the family afford the expense?

Tutoring

- Will he need special assistance you cannot learn to give yourself?
- Is an appropriate person available?

Apprenticeship

- Is he ready to begin training for life?
- Is an appropriate placement available?

Steps in Placement

Decision

Making the right decision is an important step, but it is only the first step. Carefully consider the options. Thoroughly investigate many possibilities. If the child is old enough, discuss the options with him. Don't change hastily. Fill this time with prayer. Be sensitive to the leading of the Holy Spirit.

Transition

The transition (if one is necessary) is an important time. If the child has been in public school and you decide to home educate, it may be necessary to win your child back from the disrespect for authority and the attitude of failure and laziness which he may have learned. Academics may temporarily take a back seat while you and he rediscover each other, establish spiritual strength, and develop the love for learning which is so essential. This may take a few weeks or a year or more.

Implementation

Do not take school home. Train up this child in the way he should go. Bring him along in the path that leads to his future. Academics may best be taught in the context of need. He will learn to read to gain a driver's license, learn to measure to build or cook something, learn to do math to handle his money and the bank account you help him set up (with two signatures). Early apprenticeship may be desirable rather than prolonging the agony of academic demands.

7. What Is An Adult?

**If we want to prepare our child
to be an adult,
how will we know
when they get there?**

An Adult:

- Is able to take responsibility for self.
- Is at least to some degree a self-starter.
- Is somewhat goal oriented.
- Is able to take responsibility for others.
- Knows own limits and when to ask for help.
- Is able to identify own skills and talents.
- Is literate.
- Has a basic grasp of math.
- Has some degree of people skills.
- Is an independent worker.
- Can locate information.
- Is able to ask for assistance.
- Is aware of thinking and learning processes.
- Has developed decision-making skills.
- Is somewhat flexible.
- Is somewhat organized.

Do you know any adults?

8. Discipline

This child will probably need more frequent discipline than most. Be careful that the discipline is fair and meted out carefully.

When he breaks a rule, he needs to know what he has done wrong. Whenever possible, get him to verbalize what he has done. "What is the rule? Did you do that? What is the consequence of disobeying that rule? What will happen now?"

He can only do this if the rule and the consequence were clear **before** he broke it. This is an important part of disciplining a child with special needs! Make a poster of rules with consequences clearly shown. When the child needs correction, take him to the poster and calmly lead him to see the infraction and the consequence.

Then carry out the necessary punishment or consequences. Whenever possible, use consequences rather than punishment. When possible, let the consequences be a natural outflow of the disobedience. For example, if his work is not done by three P.M. he can not go shopping with you, or he will miss 3:30 soccer practice. Or **if** he is dressed by eight A.M., he may watch a video before breakfast at 8:30.

Never discipline in anger. If you are too angry, let him know he has broken the rule and you will deal with it shortly, then step aside momentarily until you can gain control of yourself. Don't discipline two weeks after the fact; get control quickly!

Reaffirm your love for the child before, during and after the administration of discipline. He needs to know that his disobedience does not diminish your love for him and that the punishment is not because you don't love him.

If you have offended your child, deal with it!

These children are often into trouble more than most. They get on our nerves more than most. They are more sensitive than most. They may hold a grudge longer than most.

We are the adults. We are not perfect, but we have had much more experience than our children both in living and in adjusting to demands. We must seek to keep a wholesome, clean, healthy, and honest relationship with our children. They will learn far more from how we live and act with them than by what we are consciously trying to teach them.

On the other hand, our words are important. Children sometimes learn as much from what we don't say as they do from what we say.

"I was wrong. Please forgive me," are the most healing words in the world. Don't be afraid to use them!

9. Choose Your Battles Carefully!

How many rules are you willing to enforce? Have only that many rules!

Everywhere I go I see parents of toddlers who say, "Don't do that!" and turn away and allow the child(ren) to continue doing exactly what they told them not to do. They are training their child to be disobedient at a young age. I witness many of the same parents a few years later stunned that their seven or eight year old is blatantly disobedient.

If you make rules and do not enforce them, you are teaching your child to disobey and disrespect authority. Have guidelines, such as "Be loving," or "Help those in need," or "respect the property of others," and keep specific rules, such as "do not touch that", or "stop playing in the dirt," to what you are able to enforce. You will not always be there to enforce specific rules anyway, so be sure you are building character qualities in your children that respect other people and their belongings. Many behaviors which do no physical, emotional, or spiritual harm are better left unregulated.

Choose your battles carefully, then fight them to the end! You and your child will appreciate it in time.

10. Are You Looking In The Mirror?

Do your child's learning problems reflect yours and/or your husband's? If both of you are poor readers, stutter, have trouble with math, etc. your children may share your inadequacy. Learning disabilities do tend to run in families, especially among the males of the family. If you long ago accepted your level of proficiency, but expect your child to go further, you may be facing a difficult situation.

You face this choice: Accept your child where he is, find someone else who can take him further, or be willing to go with him. For instance, if both parents are poor readers, does it have to be that way forever? Perhaps you can all read aloud together for twenty minutes daily and improve together. If you're all poor in math, find a tutor who is willing to work with the family and devote some time to developing that skill. You may discover that in working together to develop the same skill, you are all strengthened and drawn together as you learn.

11. Diversification or Mass Production?

As adults, aren't the very things that make us different the same things make us interesting to each other? And isn't it those same differences that make us depend on one another?

If an adult is not good at math, he hires an accountant.

If an adult cannot type, he hires someone who can.

Why do we have to force children into molds?

I once knew a child who decided to read the entire set of encyclopedias when he was eight years old. He never did because the demands of life at home and school made it impossible for him. Another boy made the same decision at approximately the same age. He followed through! The difference? He was not forced to fit into the box called school!

Each person at an early age will show a special love and aptitude for something. If he is forced to spend his life working to gain proficiency in the things he is not good at, when will he find the time to get really good at what he loves? Are we really better off being adequate at everything when we could become really great in something?

That is not to say we should not work to improve our weaknesses. Do not give the remediation of weaknesses more importance or time than the development of aptitudes and strengths!

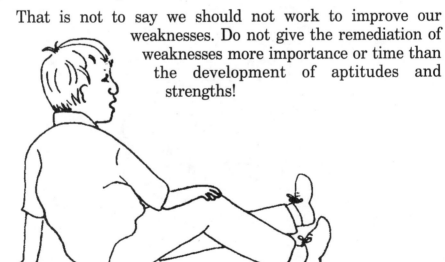

12. Depression

All of us face depression at times. As the parent or teacher of a hard-to- teach child, you are more than likely going to face times of depression. Our children who daily struggle to do what comes so easily to others are even more prone to suffer with depression. They will handle that time better if they are given some understanding of depression and some coping skills **before** they are caught in the negative thinking which is so much a part of depression.

I was a depressed child and grew into a depressed teenager. Finally in my adult years, I gained the outlook which enabled me to permanently throw off that debilitating perspective.

Part of success in conquering depression is being able to stand aside and realize that depression is common to all people and is neither permanent nor impossible to overcome. Another factor is knowing we do not struggle alone. We also need strategies to deal with the symptoms.

See Chapter 20 for more information.

13. Success

The old adage that success breeds success couldn't be truer with hard to teach children. If you are meeting resistance and apparent lack of success, **stop!** Step back and reevaluate. It may be possible to break the task down into smaller steps. Success in small steps is far preferable to failure in large chunks!

If you just can't seem to get a certain concept through, find someone else to try. Even another child may have a unique way of thinking or presenting that may help your learner grasp the problem idea.

Another possibility is backing off of a given topic or skill for a time. Weeks or months of maturation may work in your favor.

We all have a need to succeed. Children who don't find much success at school have often found success at misbehaving and found themselves caught up in a life of crime. Provide opportunities for your child to be successful in something that is wholesome and worthwhile!

Plan for success.

Pray for success.

Build success into every day.

14. "Love 'em and shove 'em!"

During my many years of teaching the philosophy that worked best was, "Love 'em and shove 'em." Just as a mother bird feeds her babies and then shoves them from the nest, we must first assure our children that they are loved and accepted, make sure they have the skills needed for independent success, and then give them the opportunity to try their wings.

Don't think of this as something to do when they are eighteen or twenty. When they are toddlers, make sure they are fed and dry and leave them alone for a time in their cribs or rooms to play or sleep. When they are a little older, give them a simple job to do and leave while they do it independently. When they are school age, make sure they have some assignments they can work out by themselves.

Love 'em and shove 'em is a daily atmosphere. Make sure they understand exactly what to do or where to find the information they need, and then leave them on their own to do it. This comes in small steps at first. Let them work independently for five minutes at first, then ten, then twenty. Gradually help them determine what needs to be done and where the information can be found and how to organize the task. Build success upon success.

Notes...

SECTION TWO

What Do I Need To DO?

Chapter
Five

Introduction
To Doing

W e can talk forever about what learning is, how to "identify" a disabled learner, and so on and so forth, but the bottom line is: How can I successfully teach this child?

Here are some preliminaries:

Get a good **physical exam**. Make sure the child is healthy and has adequate hearing, vision, and visual skills needed for school work. A word about visual skills: When a child is having difficulty concentrating on close-up work, it is not enough to test his visual acuity (Does he have 20/20 vision?). Other visual skills also need to be evaluated. They are: visual tracking, accommodation, convergence, orientation, fixation, and fusion. If your child is being tested **only** for acuity, find another evaluator! See Chapter 17 for more information.

Feed a **balanced diet** of healthy foods. Limit empty calories. Get him involved in lots of outdoor, fresh air activities. Make sure he has at least one friend. Help him to develop some skills or hobbies.

Set the stage for learning by creating a place that is child-friendly without being overwhelming - one that has good lighting, comfortable seating, appropriate learning materials conveniently stored in a non-distracting way. **Then** begin with important things first.

Realize that your child is a person, created by God for a purpose. Believe in his potential to **become** someone that you and he will like - someone who will be a blessing to himself and others.

Your child's most frustrating years will be the ones when he is forced to spend most of his waking hours struggling to learn the things that are the hardest for him. Put those skills and those years in perspective. Better yet, make a total change so that the actual academic learning is within a real life setting, a fun environment, or postponed until his learning abilities have developed. Don't let the public schools dictate the raising of your child!

Do not expect your child to struggle against failure eight to ten hours a day with no mental, physical, or emotional breaks. You couldn't do that. How do you expect him to? Learn to space difficult tasks between more pleasing and successful activities.

Be at least as tolerant of your child as you would be with a stranger. Be at least as nice to him as you would be to the child of your best friend. The only way to teach respect is to give respect!

Notes...

Chapter
Six

ABC's of Learning

A B C D E F G H I J K L M N O P Q R S T U V W X Y Z

A Accept your child with his abilities and problems.

B Believe in your child and his ability to become.

C Care about your child and his spiritual growth.

D Display your child's best work.

E Enjoy your child. This is the secret to his self-esteem.

F Figure out your child's strengths and talents.

G Give your child only the responsibilities he can handle.

H Help your child with the things he cannot do alone.

I Impress upon your child the importance of spiritual life.

J Join your child in enjoyable and meaningful activities.

K Kindle a taste for good music and literature.

L Listen to your child at two; he'll talk to you at 12.

M Model the attitudes and behavior you want to develop.

N Never belittle your child or his efforts.

O Observe your child in many situations.

P Pace your child. Help him not take on too much.

Q Question your child about what he sees, hears, and does.

R Read daily to your child from good books.

S Share your faith with your child.

T Take your child to church regularly.

U Understand that your child struggles to learn.

V Value your child's ideas.

W Worship with your child.

X eXamine your relationship with your child and with God.

Y Yield your future and that of your child to God.

Z Zero in on the eternal things!

a b c d e f g h i j k l m n o p q r s t u v w x y z

Twenty-five
Teaching Techniques
That **<u>WORK!</u>**

Teaching Techniques that Work!

1. I will thank God for this situation and pray for His guidance and blessing.

Everything really begins by accepting the situation. It is impossible for me to change anything until I know what is and accept it. I will not make a difference by demanding a total change instantly. I can only bring about change in definable steps.

If I can thank God in the midst of the mess, He may begin to alter the mess without my intervention! He may direct my efforts. He may empower me and others involved in the circumstances.

If I cannot thank God, I may limit His work in and through me. If we try to accomplish this work under our own power, we will fail.

Teach your child to accept his own limitations even as you are learning to accept yours. Teach him to depend on God, not his own ability.

Realize that your child can succeed in life. There is a place for his skills (even with his limitations) in his future.

We teach most by the attitudes we exemplify. To teach your child to rely on God, not his own skills, learn to do the same thing yourself. Let your child hear you pray for wisdom, guidance, and the skills and methods needed to teach him. Let him hear you pray for his progress, his spiritual growth, and his character development. Let your child hear you pray!

Begin at the very beginning. Line up with the commandments of God.

2. I will teach really important things first: God and the Bible.

Assess the situation: What is really important? We all have the same number of hours and minutes in a day. If it takes my child three times as long to do a reading or writing assignment as another child, is it really three times as important that he do all of that particular assignment? Is there something else that he should learn first? Is there a simpler way for him to learn, or to express that he has learned?

If it is important
that he struggle through a particular assignment,
what must he give up to make time for it?

What will it cost to demand this of my child?

What will it cost not to demand
anything of my child?

Does my child know his Father in heaven and the Bible through which God has revealed Himself to man? Does he have a relationship with God? Does he know the Word of God, both in content and application?

Does he have the social skills needed to live in our society and your family? Not all children learn social and group skills automatically. They may not interpret or even notice the quiet meanings of body language, tone of voice, facial expressions, verbal pauses, and so forth that we take for granted. It may be necessary to spend time consciously teaching and practicing many minute skills which other children pick up effortlessly.

Does he have the skills needed to survive if he lives alone? Can he cook a meal, clean the house, shop for food and clothes, launder and mend his clothes, take a phone message, budget his money, wisely spend his leisure time? Can he mow the lawn, hammer a nail, drive in a screw, replace a hinge?

57

Does he have the skills necessary to become employable? Is he prompt, organized, courteous, dependable, and so on? Can he handle schedules, finances, public transportation? Does he have the ability to make reasonable choices? Does he respect authority?

Can he follow a series of three instructions? Can he record the instructions so he can remember them long enough to follow them? Can he stick with a task long enough to finish it? Can he prioritize tasks? Can he realistically determine when someone is asking more of him than he is able to achieve?

Does he know the information and have the judgment ability needed to obtain a driver's license? Does he know the road signs and their meanings? Does he know the law and its application? Does he know the mechanics of driving? Can he make wise decisions in limited time in order to be a safe driver? Can he read a road map? Does he know how to change a tire and add gas to a car?

All of these skills may need and deserve more time for this child than for the average population. If he spends more time gaining skills others learn automatically, he must dip into time that would otherwise be used to gain academic skills. Carefully consider what he needs and look further down the road than graduation day.

What is really **first**?

Do that first!

3. I will structure routine and setting within reason.

Learning disabled students more than any others need a recognizable structure and routine in their lives. The more severe of them may almost demand a rigidity that is uncomfortable to others.

Rigidity should be avoided. If your child needs rigidity, you will have to adjust, but gently work him into a less formal structure. If you are very unstructured, you may have to do even more adjusting. Begin by having meals at approximately the same time every day. Start the day with devotions. Have an hour of structured learning tasks early in the day. After lunch every day, read a story, or recite something from the morning's lessons. Let the children enjoy a free play period outdoors just before supper. Between supper, clean up, and baths, try to have a quiet family time.

Family time might be planned to include activities which build skills and are fun while bonding the family members to each other. Enjoying a table game together is such an activity. Many skills are learned while having fun with board games! Recalling a happy event or retelling a favorite story are enjoyable activities which also encourage the development of memory, sequencing of events, and other important skills. Pick a topic, such as animals, automobiles, or tools and name all the members of that group you can think of.

End the day with Bible reading, prayer and hugs.

Have a particular place you go when certain events are to take place. Plan a specific chair or couch for listening, a different place for writing, another setting for singing. Have short phrases, hand signals, or musical tones or melodies which direct your children.

Being "in the know" has a warm feeling of belonging.

By not being too rigid, but having a familiar structure, your children have some idea of what to expect. Making a simple chart or poster (using sketches or cut out magazine pictures) to show the sequence of an average day may assist a child who is disorganized or not yet time conscious to be prepared for the little changes that go on through out the day. Have a question mark that can be inserted any time a major variation occurs.

Children who are very rigid need to be prepared even for routine change. Give a warning such as, "In five minutes we will stop and clean up so that we can eat dinner." Set a timer and follow through or be less precise in stating the time. Empty warnings encourage dawdling and excuse making. If your children are good at making excuses and dawdling, have you been making empty threats? Stop!

When you know that a certain day will not fit into the schedule (a doctor's appointment, a birthday party, a visit with grandma, etc.), be sure to tell the child early that this will be a special day. Don't spring surprises on children who deal poorly with change.

As the child matures in his ability to write or type

or draw, have him make his own schedule.

Guide him at first, but lead him to be able

to do this independently. He should be

keeping to a schedule at home where

you can guide, encourage and

remind him long before he

has to do it on the job!

Gradually increase responsibility.

4. I will prepare and maintain a relaxed, safe, positive atmosphere.

Children cannot learn in the midst of
fear, tension, or confusion.

They will not progress if they are afraid
to make a mistake.

It is our responsibility to teach our children that it is okay to fail. It is even okay to give up, but not until great effort has been directed at the problem. Giving up should usually be considered a temporary answer. A new try on a different day or after a few days or weeks of rest often results in success. We must learn and teach this principle so that our children are able to apply it to life later.

We must give genuine
encouragement and praise.

What you praise today, they will become tomorrow.

Do not give unearned praise,
but find something to praise frequently.

Tension transfers even to infants and newborns; so does a calm, positive attitude. We cannot always control what happens in our lives, but we are responsible to control our attitudes. As adults we are to set standards of attitude control.

Failures help teach us what we are not;
praise teaches us who we are.

All criticism and no praise teaches us we are worth nothing. All praise and no criticism teaches us we are god. Both are distortions of the truth.

61

Envision, expect, and predict
reasonable success and improvement.

Have encouragement on the tip of your tongue!

"I know you can't do that now,
but it will come!"

"I can see you are getting better at that."

"You are getting more skilled every day!"

"You couldn't do that many yesterday.
Good for you!"

"I am proud of the way you are working at that!"

"We'll keep watching for improvement in that!"

"Keep your eyes open; you'll see that get better!"

"I can't wait until the day when we get that right."

"It makes me really happy to see you try so hard!"

"I love to see the way you do that."

"I love the feeling I have when I see you do that!"

"Aren't you pleased when you do that?!"

"Let's show Dad (Mom, etc.) how well you can do that!"

"Let me take a picture of that moment!"

"We'll remember that for a long time!"

"Thank you for trying so hard!"

"Capture that feeling!"

5. I will be consistent in demands, discipline, expectations, and attitude.

If I do not know what I expect to teach or accomplish,
I will project confusion into the lesson.

If I punish today what I praised yesterday, I will develop a neurotic child who does not know what to do or think.

I need to define my expectations
and clearly express them to the child.

Keep behavior demands as few as possible.

Have a few general rules which cover many areas, such as:
Love one another.
In everything give thanks.
This, too, will pass.

Do all things decently and in order.
Stop, look, listen, and think.
A place for everything and everything in its place.
Always try to do your best.
Think before you speak.
Clean up and put away before you leave.
Don't go to bed angry.
Admit mistakes and ask forgiveness.

Be willing to follow your own rules!

6. I will break down tasks into achievable steps.

When we teach a child to tie his shoe, we do not show him quickly, once, and expect him to do it perfectly the next time. We show him the first step. After he has mastered that, we show him the next step and so on until he is doing the job himself. With each gain, however small, we praise him.

Analyze what you want him to do.

So many skills have become automatic for us that we may not realize how complex they really are. I saw one book that broke down the task of buttering bread into fourteen distinct steps! Most children do not need that specific information, but they may need more than we are giving. Try doing the thing yourself. Stop to ask, "What did I do? How did I do it? How can I tell (or even better, show) him what needs to be done?"

Teach him the steps.

Show him the smooth process of completion first. Then repeat showing only one step at a time. Show him what you want him to learn **today** and repeat it until he understands what you want. Let him try it. Ask him to tell you what he is doing, let him ask questions, or show him again. Don't expect him to be able to do it as fast or as well as you do without practice.

Allow adequate opportunity for practice.

Let him learn one step, then a second step. Then have him practice those two steps in sequence before teaching the third. Whenever possible, make a chart showing the steps and recording his mastery of each step. He needs to see progress to maintain interest in putting forth the effort needed to continue. Find ways to vary the practice. Do not expect him to master any skill instantly. He will need more practice than average. In all the ways you can, accept his efforts, and encourage him to stay with a job until it is mastered.

Love him as he is
while you show him what he can become!

7. I will record for the student and myself short and long term goals and achievement.

This is part of the Individualized Education Plan (IEP) which must be made for special education children receiving services from the state. See Chapter 19 for more information.

Your child needs to feel that he is making progress. You are the key to this. Find a way to record what he can do **now.** When he makes a step of progress, let him know.

Develop concrete ways of measuring progress such as:

- Count and record words read or spelled correctly.

- Move down a progressive list of math skills.

- Count words he can read in one minute.

- Make a list of all the recipes he can read or successfully prepare.

- List the books he's read, the verses he's memorized.

Keep a chart and give a star or sticker when each step is completed. Make a graph of achievement. This may record information as simple as number of books read, chapter tests passed, or arithmetic facts memorized.

Date each achievement. Call his attention to each step of progress. Celebrate milestones.

Keep a notebook for each child. Track goals, evaluations, work samples and progress. Have the child write his own evaluation occasionally. If you're really brave, let him evaluate your progress as a teacher!

Look at your long term goals. Together determine what skills are needed to achieve each one. List them and prioritize them. Begin working on the first step to each goal.

Be proud of your child!

8. I will keep assignments clear, attainable, and varied.

If a child does not know what he is to do,
he will probably not do it well!

Make sure **you** know what you expect him to do.

Clearly state your expectations.

Whenever possible, show him a finished product
or a sample of correct answers.

Model success whenever possible.

Vary the presentation, the method of practice,
and the manner of evaluation
as much as possible.

If you require oral response in reading, and written response in spelling, allow a chart, poster, or collage to be the way to answer in history or science.

Do not make the assignment so vague or so gigantic that it confuses or overwhelms. Break large or long term projects into small achievable steps. Allow him to ask questions until he feels that he can succeed alone. Have him retell the assignment in his own words.

Be sure he is capable of doing what you are asking. This can be tricky, but the better you know your child, the easier it becomes. If you're not sure, encourage him to try. Ask him to work as far as he can. Be available to watch how much effort he puts into it. If he really seems to be trying and isn't making headway, find another way to approach the task.

Work with your child. Consider yourselves members of the same team. Do not allow yourself to get caught in a power struggle, or to be pitted against him. Work together!

9. I will reward small achievements.

Some children feel they never receive rewards because it takes so much longer for them to reach a goal than others. Small achievements may deserve only small rewards, but they do need rewards. That doesn't mean we have to keep candy or trinkets always in front of them. Nor does it mean we have to be forced into giving awards every time a child spells a word. Rewards are best when unexpected and pleasant.

Many children are motivated by stickers or a symbol stamped on a paper. Consider a marble or new postage stamp for a collector, a trip to the library, or a treat to share with a pet. Ten minutes for cuddle time, back yard play, computer time or something the child enjoys is fine. Sometimes a hug, a touch on the shoulder, or a smile and a wink is reward enough. Try reducing the amount of work or practice. For instance, if the child gets a perfect math paper one day, have him do every other problem the next. Be sure your rewards encourage harder work next time.

Be careful to give something that is treasured by the recipient. When I was ten, a reward for me would have been a whole day to read books; that may be a torture for another child! Make sure the reward is appropriate for the achievement. Do not give a weekend camping trip for the spelling of one word unless it was very difficult to achieve! On the other hand, if he spent a month mastering printing his name, don't offer him a peanut.

Praise small bits of real progress. Praise must always be genuine and enthusiastic! If there is absolutely no progress, praise the effort put forth and assure him that progress will come. Look for small evidences of progress and call them to his attention with praise. Occasionally plan rewards just because! We do not want our children to begin to think that they can or must earn our love. They need to know that our love is not dependent on their performance or achievement.

10. I will give limited choices to allow the student to have some control.

I will limit the choices to what he can control and gradually increase the amount of responsibility I expect.

Everyone needs to feel some control over their own lives. Children do not always make wise choices when left to their own. Making wise choices is a skill to be learned in small steps like any other skill. At first offer a choice between two:

- Would you like to do math now or after lunch?
- Would you like to wear the blue plaid or the green shirt?
- Would you rather practice spelling by writing the words with markers or chalk?
- Later offer more options.
- Would you like read a story to me, listen to a tape, or read quietly to yourself?
- Would you rather do your page of math before lunch, after snack time, or right now?

  When you finish cleaning your room, would you like to play outside, read a book, or ride your bike?

Never offer a choice when there is none!

Don't say, "Do you want to go to bed?" unless the choice is **really** up to the child.

11. I will use multi-sensory presentations which involve the learner.

Multi-sensory approaches are more than see, say, and write. It is more than using a tape recording with an auditory learner and a picture with a visual learner. For more about learning styles, see Chapter Twelve.

Multi-sensory approaches should involve the learner through his hands, his eyes, his mind, his heart, his ears, his touch, and his voice. Multi-sensory may involve manipulation of blocks, cards, or pieces of paper. It may involve rhythmic repetition, musical concepts, and large muscle movement. It should always engage the brain to understand and whenever possible, give the heart opportunity to feel and to enjoy. When the whole person is involved in the learning, the lesson will be remembered longer.

Use at least two senses in a meaningful context for the best learning. Whenever possible, put information in the context of a story. Use words that are easy to picture. Put the concept, not just the practice into rhythm and music.

Be wary of programs that say they are multi-sensory and turn out to be see, say, and write. Not many learning disabled children are thrilled with this type of practice. If they hate the practice, they are not likely to learn or enjoy the skill.

Multi-sensory involves the whole person.

Be careful not to overwhelm or confuse.

Some children quickly reach over-load in visual or auditory stimulus. Be aware of limits and be wise enough to limit input **before** it disrupts or overwhelms. Avoid circumstances which are generally over-stimulating such as malls in the Christmas season, noisy pizza parlors, and busy playgrounds.

12. I will allow frequent physical and mental breaks.

Children with short attention spans are often overwhelmed by the necessity of sitting in one place and listening to the same voice. They need to stop and refocus more frequently than we do. Provide opportunity to break, but also provide **directed and assisted return to work**!

Take a wiggle moment, take a brief run outside, or allow a five minute bathroom break. Have a snack, tell a joke, or call attention to progress and success. Do a song with movement, stand and stretch, or change the subject and manner of presentation. When possible, move to a different setting for the break, so that a return to the work setting signals a return to work attitude. This should be done every five to fifteen minutes for younger or "attention deficit" children, every half hour or hour for older children who can handle more.

When the break is over, it is important to assist the children in returning to work by stating calmly what you expect and then showing them through your voice and actions what to do. This step is vital to prevent chaos. My husband once took over my class for a week during my illness. When I returned he was amazed at how swiftly the children obeyed. I merely stated what I expected them to do and they did it. Obviously I had already spent time training them to know that if I said it, I meant it!

Children need breaks, but they also need assistance in returning to on-task behavior. At the beginning of the break, set a timer to remind them when it is time to go back to work. Have them practice their response to the timer until it automatically signals a return to control and concentration.

Help your child develop good habits.

13. I will provide frequent reviews in different learning styles.

Review does not always have to be recite or write.

- Try graphing information or making a chart.

- Have the children make up review questions; then discuss their questions and be sure the important points are included.

- Let them listen to a summary while they draw.

- Play a game fashioned after a television quiz show using review questions.

- Use review questions along with a board game — a right answer wins a move.

- Have one child teach another. He has to know it well to teach!

- Illustrate the important truths through stories or anecdotes that make the concept come alive in word pictures.

- Next time see if the child can retell the word picture, draw it, or offer one of his own.

- Have the child draw illustrations or diagrams of the main points and explain them to someone.

- Have the student(s) try to retell the important points in as few words as possible!

- Have him draw the main point of the reading lesson, spell orally, write the math answers, make a collage for history, and a chart for science.

Use your imagination! If you lack imagination, buy it! There are many good books on the market to assist you in this. It is a hot topic!

14. I will allow for a variety of expression.

Here are some ideas for varying expression:

Have the child:

- Do a demonstration of the learned skill. Reproduce information by drawing, diagramming, or making a model. Write a poem or song. Make a poster, a collage, or a diorama. Making a replica may force concentration on details not considered important at first glance.

- Even an older child can point to an answer or move something to indicate their response. This may be very important to remember if the child is limited in motor functioning and unable to write with ease. Use an electric board where the correct answer rings a bell or lights a light.

- Make a puppet and present a show to other students. Make a tape recording similar to a newscast. Video tape a drama about the topic. Write or dictate a letter to a person of the future, a relative, or a historical hero. Pretend you participated in a historical event and write your diary.

- Create a board game which reviews the content. Make up a crossword or wordsearch puzzle. Make a mini-book, a chart, or a graph. Build a working model. Teach another child a mastered skill.

- Write, produce, and act in a play about the subject. Recite the facts while you do jumping jacks. Spell a word in sign language. Produce clay models to illustrate a point.

There are really hundreds of ways to express information. Just make sure you point out any important facts they may have missed. We should not limit a student's expression to fill in the blanks and multiple choice.

Be creative and encourage creativity in the child!!

15. I will relate the unknown to previously known information.

When information comes to us in a vacuum, it is usually rejected by the spirit and by the intellect.

To be remembered, it must be understood.

To be understood, it must be important.

To be important, it must relate to something that is known, understood, and remembered already.

For example, when you teach fractions, bring in a real object. Cut it in half in front of the child. Show the child how to write 2/2 and 1/2 and what each of those symbols mean. Then cut each piece in half two more times. Show them 8/8, 1/8, and other possibilities. Immediately show them adding 1/8 plus 1/8 and subtracting 4/8 take away 1/8. Ask them which they'd rather have, 1/2 or 1/8. They will quickly figure out that the smaller the number on the bottom the larger the piece and the larger the number on top the more pieces. Then segment an orange and figure out how to write the correct fraction. The next day do a few simple problems based on what they saw. The next day give more related experience. They will begin to understand fractions because they have been presented in a way that has meaning in their own lives!

Most skills can be introduced in this hands on, relevant way. Decide what you really want them to learn, where they will need that information, and how you can show its usefulness as you teach it. Use real life application in introductions, practice, summaries, and reviews!

16. I will not teach what I will have to unteach.

Too many curriculums are teaching an untruth temporarily. Try to avoid those curriculums and that problem. Do not teach reading and writing sentences before you teach capital letters because a capital letter is needed at the beginning of **every** sentence.

This seems so obvious to me, but many people don't notice, or they notice and do it anyway.

Don't speak in absolutes (all or never) because if **one** exception is found, we are wrong and our children have genuine cause to not believe us in the future. We are not perfect, we will make mistakes. But we can eliminate many by following this one simple rule:

Don't teach untruth!

Don't give your children opportunity
to doubt that there is a truth.

Don't give them opportunity to wonder if you are able to
identify the truth when you see it.

Seek out the truth and teach it!

Foundational Truths:

God is.

He has revealed Himself to man.

The Bible is the chief source of His revelation.

God is righteous, holy, loving, forgiving, and just.

He made man and recognizes man's need.

God has provided a Savior in the Person of Jesus Christ.

The work of Jesus is finished.

The blessings of God are available to all who ask.

God will not force Himself or His Son on anyone.

Man is naturally sinful.

Man has no power to remove the consequences of sin.

He needs a Savior.

All the blessings of God are available for the asking.

The blessings of God cannot be earned or paid for.

Response to God is not a choice.

The only choice is **how and when** to respond to God.

There are other truths in the physical and spiritual world. Life's adventure is discovering them!

17. I will be as practical as possible.

When you teach a subject, try to relate it to a need in the child's life. If it is not needed yet, try to make them feel the future need. If you cannot, perhaps you should wait.

We learn best what we are interested in! Help your children be interested. When possible, move from their natural play (You did leave time for that, didn't you??) to the topic you want them to learn.

Teach counting in relation to stuffed animals on the shelf, plates needed to set the table, or blocks to build a tower.

Relate fractions to sharing toys. You have ten cars and a friend comes to play. He gets half of them. How many do you have left? If a third child comes to play, how many will you each give him to play with?

Teach measuring with cups and pints during bath or water play, pouring from one container to another, or while cooking.

Use money skills to set up a budget.

Center development of language skills around toys, writing letters, doing housework, or keeping a journal.

Science can be a natural outflow of things that happen around the house. Baking a cake is a chemical reaction. Why does soap remove dirt from your hands? What causes rain?

Encourage curiosity and wonder regarding the creation of God. Everything God created reveals an aspect of who He is!

Reading biographies is the best way to teach history.

Teach **first** the skills needed to cope with normal living (danger and bathroom signs when they are young, budgeting and checkbook skills later, etc.). Then go on to the "fluff".

18. I will give the big picture in the early stages of learning.

Many people who have difficulty learning cannot understand the pieces until they see the whole. When we give them a hundred phonics facts or history dates we have created a problem for them. We would not give them a five hundred piece puzzle and hide the box lid to speed their learning. Why do we give them so many seemingly unrelated pieces of information and expect them to extrapolate the whole from the pieces? Probably because that was the way we were taught!

Whenever possible in presenting a new topic, show the whole first.

Then relate each piece to the whole.

Show a block design, take it apart, and then ask the child to reconstruct it. Or put it back together and ask the child to make another just like it. Let him watch the whole process before you ask him to try it.

In an art lesson, show a finished project. Better yet, show several ways to carry out the instructions or method. For instance, show a finger painting, then try finger painting on typing paper, magazine pages, a plastic bag, sandpaper, wax paper, aluminum foil, and a brown paper bag. Observe the differences.

When teaching phonics, show how stories are made of sentences, sentences are made of words, and words are made of letters. Then teach the letter sounds!

In teaching history, summarize the period **before** you teach the details. Use a time line. Show a chart of related happenings within a given time frame. Talk about how religious events affect art, music, and politics.

These children are usually least able to put the whole together by looking at many pieces, **so do it for them!**

19. I will give the student a purpose for learning.

If I can't think of a purpose for learning it, I won't teach it.

A purpose for learning. Why are we teaching each skill, each fact? If our reason is that it will be asked on a test, maybe we need to rethink. These are children who will need to put forth more time and effort to learn almost everything they attempt. They cannot take in as much information or master as many skills as some other children. Therefore we must carefully choose what we ask of them.

Teach reading so the child
can read the Scriptures by himself.

Teach math so the child
can take care of his toys and his money.

Teach history to save a child
from repeating someone else's mistakes.

Teach language so the child
can clearly communicate the truth.

Teach a foreign language in order to
communicate with a pen pal or missionary.

Teach science so the child can marvel
at God's creativity and power in nature.

Teach safety so the child will be able to protect
himself and serve others in time of need.

Teach household skills so the child
will be able to live on his own one day.

Teach music and art as expressions of creativity, as leisure
activities, and to enhance appreciation for beauty.

Determine *why* before you decide *what* to teach!

20. I will seek to make the information relevant and interesting.

If you want me to learn division, give me twelve cookies and three friends! Show me that it has meaning in **my** life.

Studies show that information is best assimilated and skills are best developed when taught within the normal context of day to day living. Home-educating provides the natural opportunity for learning within a context of reality, but in too many cases, parents bring school home instead of taking the child out of school.

I will learn the importance of measuring carefully
if I am cooking, sewing, or doing carpentry work.

I will quickly learn to add or subtract if I have to keep track of
the money I earn and spend, my tithe and my savings.

I will learn pleasing color combinations
when I choose my clothes.

I will learn to read if someone writes me letters.

I will become interested in history through the life of someone I
appreciate, understand, and identify with.

I will learn writing and spelling skills when
I am recording information that is important to me
or I want to communicate with someone who is far away.

I will learn hygiene when I care what someone else thinks.

I will learn to look up information when
I realize that I don't have all the answers.

I will learn to sing when I realize it is pleasing to Someone.

Make it relevant! Make it count!

21. I will show the student his progress at frequent intervals.

This is **very important!** We all need to feel that the effort we put forth is accomplishing something. Children are no different!

**You cannot show the child his progress
unless you have a system
of keeping track
of his achievements!**

Here are some simple suggestions:

- Keep a chart and add stars, check marks, initials, or stickers for each step of achievement.

- Keep an anecdotal record with one line each day in each topic. (For ease of comparing, keep each topic for each child on a different sheet of paper.)

- Have a list of the steps to success and date the mastery of each step.

- Photograph and date each step of progress.

- Make a video of your child. Each month add to it and watch last month's segment.

- Make a bulletin board with many parts missing (a worm with many segments, a tree with many leaves). Add a segment for each fact learned, book read, verse memorized, etc.

- Let him earn a penny for each word he learns to spell or fact he remembers. When he has $2.00, take him to the store.

- Ask your student how he would like to keep track of his progress! He may have a better idea!

22. I will stop thinking grade level and grades and begin to think in terms of learning and progress.

How did we get along without grade levels and grades until the nineteenth century? Simple! As each step was mastered, we taught the next one!

Students with learning differences are least likely to progress evenly or according to someone's schedule. When they are constantly compared to an impossible timeline of achievement, they easily become frustrated and overwhelmed. This isn't to say that we do away with standards, we just don't put an unrealistic expectation on the amount of time it may take to achieve.

On the other hand, we do need to expect achievement and mastery of subjects. Children tend to live up, or down, to our expectations. Be realistic, project positive goals and their achievement. Record progress. Stop worrying about an arbitrary grade level or report card.

I have some text books from the nineteenth century. The grade level expectations were more difficult than our public schools today. Students began with the primer whether they were five or fiften and continued in it until they had mastered the material. The *Federalist Papers* were written for rural farmers of 1787, but today's college graduate would find them difficult to read! Designations of grades and grade levels are quite arbitrary, change with the culture, and are therefore fairly meaningless! The scriptures warn us against measuring ourselves among ourselves by ourselves. Grade levels, grades, and standardized achievement tests are just that.

There is really only one standard worthy of the name, and that is the life of Jesus!

It is informative to know that you have correctly spelled 95% of the 110 words which have a short vowel sound. It is not informative to know that a child got an A in math in the first grade or a B in a college course in physics. Grades cannot tell what was learned or even what material was covered!

Be careful not to be sucked into doing something because that is the "way it has always been done." How long is always? Do you see achievement tests in the Old Testament? Or report cards in the New? Did Jesus ever come and say, "Congratulations! You are now ready for second grade skills!" Of course not! He presented the content of what he wanted to teach in stories that anyone could relate to. He took a selected few into his inner circle and related to them one or two at a time. He taught by letting them walk with him, listen to him, participate in life with him. He taught until they learned. He taught to his death. He taught in a context of need and interest.

Instead of grades and grade levels,
compare yourself and your children
to the standard of Christ.

When we fail, we lean on Him.

When we succeed, we give Him thanks.

23. I will concentrate on disciplining attitude more than behavior.

When a child spills milk, we may determine whether it was deliberate for attention or accidental because of lack of motor control. We respond accordingly. If it was attitude, discipline that; if it was motor control, teach the child to clean up his own mess. We need to do the same thing in other learning situations.

Look beyond the action to the attitude.

If we only correct behavior, children get the impression that **they** aren't important - only their behavior is important. They can become great actors to win our approval with no change of heart. Or they may rebel against the meaningless of behavior demands. We need to be careful not to become behaviorists.

God is far more interested with the condition of the heart! God created people with potential for good or evil depending on their attitude, character, and relation to Him. Perfect behavior without a change of heart is not pleasing to Him. When the heart is right, God forgives even major behavior flaws as exemplified in the life of David in the Old Testament.

Your own heart must be right before you can lead your child into a right relation to God. Keeping our attitudes and relation right with God helps us focus on the truly important aspects of our child's education.

Developing healthy and wholesome attitudes is of major importance, but it is only possible in the context of a right relationship with God!

We need to learn to look beyond the surface behavior to the attitudes of the heart.

24. I will teach the student to cope and compensate as I attempt to train the skills he will need in life.

To cope means to handle the reality of the problem. To compensate means to find another way to solve the problem.

A child who has poor motor control needs to learn to be responsible for cleaning up the messes which inevitably result. A child with poor auditory skills needs to think about carefully watching every step of a demonstration and taking notes which he can later verbalize. Weak visual skills make listening skills more important. Poor memory skills make note-taking of paramount importance! Help the child accept himself and his limitations as you train him to work through other avenues.

If you discover a child learns best through the auditory channel, **do not limit his learning experiences to his good channel - or fill up his time with training the weak channel!** Strike a balance. Do not spend more than fifty percent of your time remediating a weak or lost skill or teaching through one learning channel. Teach through as many means as possible. He will pick up the information through his strongest channel while he builds skill in the weaker one.

Use every opportunity to show the child examples of people who have succeeded in life in spite of great odds. Help him to look realistically at his own abilities and inabilities. Teach him to cope with the depression and frustration that inevitably come with his limitations.

Teach your child the real source of strength and show him how you rely on God's strength in your daily struggles.

25. I will thank God for this situation and pray for His guidance and blessing.

Prayer and acceptance is the first step and the last.

Put this child's learning problem into perspective!

It is not life threatening.

The problem can be handled.

If responded to correctly,
you and your child will be strengthened
in your relationship to each other and
in your individual relationships with God.

God does have a purpose for this person!

Keep that thought ever in front of both of you!

God has a purpose for every person!

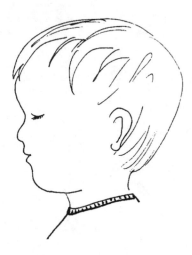

Notes...

TEENY TINY
TEACHING TIPS

T he following pages include helpful hints in many areas of life. They are bits and pieces gleaned from many years of working with children and families. I pray that you will find something that meets you where you are and helps you get where you want to go!

Foods —

When a child doesn't like a food he has tasted, accept that, but project positive feelings in the future. Remind him that when he was tiny, he liked pablum, warm milk, etc. As he grows up, his tastes change and something he doesn't like today he may develop a taste for in the future.

Cut or serve the food to make it look fun.

Feed small amounts of new foods to children even when they are very young.

Feed one finger food at every meal to build dexterity.

Let the child help prepare food. Even a young child can spread jam or put raisins on peanut butter.

Keep sauces separate and let the child dip vegetables in it.

Try to include one favorite food with each meal.

Don't project your food preferences onto your children.

Be flexible, but don't become your child's slave! If he likes ketchup or cinnamon on everything, will it really hurt?

Remember, at each meal tots need only a tablespoon of protein per year of age. Don't force eating as much as an adult!

Children need snacks. Make them as nutritious as possible. Fruit, fruit shakes, frozen fruit ices, yogurt, vegetables with a dip, and crackers with cheese or peanut butter make good snacks. Try mixing several unsugared cereals with a few peanuts, cinnamon, and raisins in a plastic bag. Shake together to blend flavors. Serve as munchies. Or use the cereals mixed with popcorn, pretzels, and peanuts.

Household —

Have a schedule posted. This may be as simple as seven symbols in sequence: dressing, breakfast, school or chores, lunch, school or play, supper, play and devotions. Don't box yourself in rigidly, but give your life some recognizable form.

Dressing, shoes: Draw smiley faces on the inside arch of each shoe. When the shoes are on the correct feet, the smiles will be looking at each other.

Dressing, coats: An easier way: Lay coat upside-down in front of child. Have him slide his arms through the coat into the sleeves and then raise the coat up over his head.

Table setting: In proper positions, trace plate, silver, glass, and napkin on 11"x18" posterboard. Color and cover with clear contact paper. Make enough for the family on one color posterboard, and some for guests on another.

Left/Right —

Use a permanent marker to put smiley faces on the inside arch of shoes. If shoes are on the correct feet, the smiley faces will kiss each other. You may also want to label them left and right.

Let him wear a ring on his right hand.

Two fisted approach: Make two fists. Put ring areas of fists together with thumbs extended upward. Look at them. You see in front of you a "b" and a "d." They are in alphabetical order. If the thumbs are a headboard and footboard, the hands also form a bed. If you say "bed" as you look at them from left to right the word bed will help you remember.

Put a green dot in the left margin of the paper and a red dot in the right margin. Do this at the beginning of every line if necessary. Green means go, so you start on the left. Red means stop, so you finish on the right.

Motor —

Balance: Cover a plank with carpet. Attach a two by two to the bottom, horizontally in the middle. Have child stand on top and rock back and forth to rhythm or music.

Balance: Have child walk the wide side of a two by four. When he is pretty good, bury it or support it so the 2" side is up. When he masters that, have him do other things as he walks across: touch his toes, turn around, look at a target, etc.

Ball Skills: Rolling a ball is easier than tossing one. For catch, start with a partially deflated beach ball. As skills increase, gradually add air. When that is mastered, gradually decrease the size of the ball and increase the distance between players.

Skipping: A skip is a step-hop in fast sequence. Master hopping (on each foot!) first. Then step, hop on the same foot, switch feet and repeat. Do it slowly until a rhythm is established. Some researchers say a child is ready to learn to read when he can skip.

Jumping Jacks: Start with legs only. Feet together. Hop out. Hop back. Build speed and rhythm. Then do hands only. Slap sides, clap overhead. Develop each of these skills to a rhythm. Then hop out as you swing hands up. Try to clap at the same moment the feet land. Then hop back and swing hands back. Try to slap sides when the feet land.

Fine Motor —

Start in infancy, letting your child pick up peas, green beans, dry cereal, etc., to eat. With an older child, encourage eating popcorn, grapes, or other treats one piece at a time.

Use clay or play dough. Encourage rolling, patting, stretching, making balls, etc.

Have him sort buttons, coins, or bolts and screws. Muffin tins and ice cube trays make good sorting trays.

Encourage drawing. Have him draw while looking at real objects. Have him verbalize as he looks and draws.

Allow drawing with many materials: chalk, marker, dry erase, pen, crayon. Use a variety of papers: typing, lined, magazines, bright colors, construction, sandpaper, etc.

Use stencils. Choose large heavy ones of basic shapes like a circle and square at first. Crepe rubber puzzles make wonderful stencils. Have him trace inside the stencil at first, them have him trace around the cut out shape. Gradually decrease the size and increase the complexity of the shape. Have him trace a shape, then try immediately, while the feel is fresh, to reproduce its shape and size in a drawing of his own.

Visual Perception —

Use patterns with blocks. First have child build the blocks on top of the pattern. When this is easy, have him build beside the pattern. Later, stand the pattern in front of him and have him build the design on the table. Gradually increase the distance between the child and the pattern.

Use interlocking stacking brick type blocks to create a pattern for him to copy. Use only two to four blocks at first. Increase the number of blocks and complexity of design as he is successful.

Use a geoboard. This is an 8" square board with nails standing up at 1" intervals. You need two - one for your design and one for the child to use. Use colored rubber bands to outline shapes which the child will copy on his board. (Plastic geoboards may be purchased from school supply stores.) Make the shapes very simple at first using only one rubber band. At first you verbalize important characteristics, later have him verbalize.

Auditory Perception —

Read aloud rhymes, tongue twisters, and repetitive and alliterative works. Laugh and enjoy the sounds.

Identify and mimic animal and machine sounds.

Set a timer and take a two minute break when it rings. Gradually soften the sound by putting a pillow over it or moving it further away.

Tell riddles and jokes. Have him repeat the punch line.

Tell a two sentence story. Ask him to retell or repeat it. Gradually increase the length of the story.

Cutting Skills —

The child may need to start with simple spring scissors (snippers) which open automatically.

Begin by snipping pieces off a strip of paper less than an inch wide and five inches long. Use the snips in a collage as tree leaves.

Use scissors with play dough or bread dough.

Gradually widen the strip until the child has to open the scissors twice to get across. Use the longer strips in a picture as hair on a person or animal.

Pencil Grip —

Teach him the right way to hold a pencil when he is two and first picks up a crayon. It's far easier to make a habit than to break one!

Grips too far up the pencil? Give him short pencils!

Grips too far down the pencil? Wrap a row of masking tape around, so he'll hold it above the tape. If he holds on the tape, put it where you want him to hold it. Or buy little rubber contoured pencil grips in his favorite color.

Handwriting —

Left/Right Problems? Put a green dot in the left margin of each line and a red dot in the right margin. Green for start, red for stop.

Trouble finding top or correct side of paper? Use pen that will not bleed through to put a black dot in the upper right.

Trouble staying on the line? Trace the bottom line with a crayon in the child's favorite color. Press hard. Teach him to draw lines from top to bottom. When pencil touches the crayon line, there is a different feel.

Use paper marked in 1" squares to help develop writing skills. Write the alphabet, printing one letter in each square.

Is your child nine or ten and *still* finds writing difficult? Teach correct keyboarding and word processing skills.

Giving Directions —

Be sure you have the child's attention by making eye contact. If he isn't listening and looking, he can't hear or see.

Speak distinctly and clearly.

Be specific. Use simple terms. This is not the time to use long complicated sentences.

Give one instruction. See that it is followed through. Gradually increase the number of steps of introduction and the amount of time before checking to see that it has been carried out as the child gains skill. If he begins to fail, back up to one or two instructions and build up again.

When possible, show as you explain. Use words that are easy to picture. For example, "Do you know where your red elephant is? Put this on the same shelf."

If a list is long, make a note for the child. Number the left and make a single symbol (or let the child do it) for each task. Have him check them off as he finishes them.

Memorizing —

Start when very young memorizing scripture, simple songs, and letter or number sequences.

Enjoy reciting together. Small children love repetition. Older ones enjoy it only if they learn to when they are young, or if it is very silly or has some alliteration.

Play audio tapes of Scriptures, songs, and information during quiet times. Repeat important ones frequently. Repeat the verse frequently, each time leaving out an agreed upon word. Think the missing word.

Write a verse on the board. Repeat it as you erase a word. Repeat, erasing one word at a time until there are no words left and you are saying it from memory.

Allow him to move or do exercises as he memorizes.

Use visual and auditory repetition. When possible add hand or body motions, rhythm, or melody. They aid memory.

Reading —

Read to him, read with him, read in front of him, read, read, read. Let him know you enjoy reading.

Read just enough of a book to get him interested and stop at a **good** place. Say, "Won't it be great when you can finish this by yourself?"

Let him read books which are below his achievement level. Call it his enjoyment level.

Read to him, but when you come to a word he knows, point to it and have him say it. Go on quickly without losing continuity. Later, have him read every third paragraph or page.

When he reads to you, have him point to the words he cannot read and you tell him quickly. Save struggling and sounding out for another time.

Let him read to children much younger than himself.

Have him find a word (sentence) in the newspaper or Bible or encyclopedia that he can read without help.

Spelling —

Teach spelling in word families (at, bat, fat, sat, etc.). Teach mastery of each family. Show the same word family in larger words (atmosphere, battery, saturate). Don't expect mastery of these harder words, but read them with the student two days in a row, then let him try to spell them.

Learn two word families, then mix words from both. Learn a third family, then mix the words from all three. Do not teach on Monday for a test on Friday. Keep incorporating old words in new dictation sentences and assignments. Don't just memorize a list of words; teach principles.

Have him start a spelling file box. Use alphabetical dividers. Make a card for each letter or for two letter combination that may begin a word: ab, ac, ad, ae, af, ag, ah, ai, etc. There will be no aj (no pk, or sf, etc.). Make only plausible combinations. When he asks you to spell a word, have him bring you the right card and write the word on the card as you spell it. Next time he may find it on the card and not have to ask you!

Choose five words from his spelling file box each week. Add them into all of his writing and spelling assignments.

Make 2" x 6" strips of construction paper or poster board. Print the letters or his spelling words in large letters. Trace them with a fine line of glue. Allow to dry several hours or overnight without touching. They are good for tracing with the finger. Have him say the letter or spell the word as he traces it to increase memory. (Or, to increase sensory input for tracing, you may want to sprinkle them with sand while they are wet.)

Use the dried glue words to make a crayon rubbing. Put one word under a sheet of paper. Rub the side of a crayon (paper removed) on the paper over the word. The word will appear on the paper. Draw a picture of the word or use it in a sentence and then do it again. Fill the page.

Math —

Can't write the answer? Get numeral stamps.

Use paper marked in 1" squares or grid for counting and printing numerals.

Keeping in columns: Use one inch or one-half inch grid paper. Print one numeral in each square.

Use peanuts, raisins, popcorn, or cereals for counting, adding, multiplying or dividing. At the end of every session do subtraction and eat them! They will love subtraction!

To teach area and perimeter, walk the perimeter of a play area. Say with the children, "We are walking the perimeter. Then we will play in that area." Point to the area within the perimeter you are walking.

After the above exercise, use paper marked in 1" squares for practicing area and perimeter. Have the child cut out squares and rectangles of different sizes (always evenly on the lines which form the squares). Then have the child figure and write both the perimeter and the area on the back.

Cut strips of squares from paper marked in 1" squares. Have the child color in some of the squares in each strip. The next day, figure the fraction for each strip. For example, if there are four squares and three are colored, the fraction is 3/4. The next day, see if there are other ways to name any of the fractions. For example, 2/4 could also be named 1/2, because both sides are the same size.

When multiplying by two or more digits, consider each digit a member of a team. Each team member has to play against all members of the other team. When a new player steps up to play, he puts a zero down for each member of his team that already played. For example, when multiplying 654 x 321, 1 plays first against 4, 5, and 6. When 2 begins, he moves to the next line and first puts down a zero because one member of his team has played. Then he plays 4, 5, and 6 and writes the answer moving left from the zero. When 3 plays, he writes his score on the next line and begins with 2 zeros because two team members have played. Finally add up the scores to find the team's total score.

Post a multiplication chart across the room or out of sight. Except on a test, allow the child to walk to the chart and look for the answer to any fact he doesn't know. He should recite the fact with its answer as he walks back to his seat

Relate math to the real world. Measure for cooking or building a treehouse. Count by threes or fives.

Problem Solving Techniques —

Draw a picture.	Guess and test.
Make a table.	Make a graph.
Act out the problem.	Substitute simpler numbers.
Draw a diagram.	Make a model.
Write an equation.	Look for a pattern.
Estimate, experiment.	Work the problem backwards.
Think logically.	Make a list of known facts

Use objects to act out the problem.

General —

Have an on going project that you work on a little bit every week and finally finish in a month or a year. Today's children are too frequently led to believe that all of life's problems are solved in twenty minute segments between commercials. Strike a compromise between no deadlines (nothing gets done) and stringent deadlines that overstress.

If you are a mom, you are not just a mom. You are a woman, a wife, a neighbor, a shopper, a friend. Your child is not just a child with learning problems. He is also many other things. Help him see that and enjoy who he is.

When you exercise, you build strength slowly. Mental exercise is much the same. We can't progress without effort or continue struggling when there is no visible progress.

If you see frustration coming, stop and rethink what you are doing. Is there another way to present the idea? Is there a different person who could teach it? Would waiting be better?

Whenever possible stop when your child is having fun so that he (and you) will be eager to begin again.

Carry a timer in your pocket. Use it to challenge. How many toys can get in the box in one minute? How clean can the living room get in two minutes? How many math problems can you finish in five minutes? Use it to reward. You've worked hard for fifteen minutes! You may have a two minute wiggle break. It builds time consciousness and limits struggle time. Anybody can struggle with a hard task for two minutes!

Use a metal cookie sheet with magnetic letters or numerals. Spell words. Do math problems. Design with shapes.

Use a shallow plastic tray with a lid for a writing tray. Put in a half inch of salt or sand. Have the child draw or print letters or numbers in it. Gently shake to erase. When boredom sets in, change to hot chocolate mix or cinnamon sugar! Right answers get a lick!

Keep a diary or journal and encourage your child to do the same. It is rewarding in many ways.

Purchase school type work books in discount chain stores. Most children enjoy working in them or playing school, and they build skills at the same time.

Expand your own thinking to allow for many ways to do or think about a given topic.

Collect magazines and make a scrapbook on a topic of interest to the child. Help him make labels.

Join 4-H or another group which encourages children to participate, experiment, relate, and learn.

Teach your child the "wow" of learning and allow him the thrill of discovery. Don't provide all the answers - or prevent all the problems.

Purchase a package of page protectors. Put any page in it and use a dry erase marker, china marker, or overhead projector pen on the plastic to make the page reusable many times. Especially helpful for math facts!

Take the time to look and explore obscure things that might be missed, like the empty lot in your neighborhood, the weeds growing at the edge of the yard, or the elderly neighbor who never comes out of his house.

Take time for yourself and allow your child to have time by himself. Many great thoughts are born in the quiet of a moment alone with God.

Emphasize cans, not can't! If he has no hands, he can play soccer. If he can't write, he can type. Learn to substitute.

Having fun and learning something new together will draw you together. Or let him learn something and teach you!

Keep a loose leaf notebook each year for each child. Keep a sample of his work in each subject. Have him make a list of all the books he reads and the ones you read to him. Have him write a daily or weekly journal. Keep a record of verses memorized and prayer requests. Keep some of his drawings, cards or letters he received, ticket stubs, etc. Wonderful for remembering later and enjoying accumulated progress!

Find ways to make your child right and not wrong. If he says he lives in the country of Indiana, say, "Yes, you live in the country and you live in Indiana. Indiana is the state you live in and you live in the country or rural area. The name of the country you live in is the United States of America. Indiana is only one of the states in the United States of America."

Never, ever, ever belittle your child or his efforts.

Always project future success.

Notes...

SECTION THREE

WHERE DO I START?

Chapter
Nine

Begin at the
Very Beginning

Down to Basics

To increase in wisdom,
in stature,
and in favor with God
and man
Luke 2:52

Determine Your Priorities
and Set Goals

Spiritual

I will introduce my child to God and His Truth. I will emphasize that God created him as he is for a purpose. He can't do everything well, but he can do some things well! I will take him step by step through obtaining and developing a relationship with the Lord. I will teach him how to use the Bible for support, encouragement, strength, and wisdom.

Emotional

I will assure my child that he is loved and valuable and that, with God's help, we can handle anything God allows to come our way. I will teach him to handle failure as well as success. I will accept his emotions while I assist him in handling emotional outbursts. I will teach him an appropriate way to handle the frustrations and energies that are associated with his learning problems. I will be there for him in his times of depression and exultation.

Social

I will provide opportunity for my child to have at least one good friend (not necessarily his own age) to relate to and have fun with. I will encourage him to be involved in whatever type of group activities he can successfully handle. I will assist him in developing recreational skills which are fun for one person as well as skills with a single friend and with a team.

104

Physical

I will encourage and provide opportunity for my child to develop at least one physical skill as far as he is able. I will allow him the time it takes to use the energy that abounds in his body. I will be sure that he develops in a solo sport that he can excel in without the added challenge of group dynamics. I will provide opportunity for limited group sports and increase that as his skill in handling competition increases.

Academic

I will set a few attainable goals and praise his successes without comparing him to others his age. I will communicate and record the goals and steps he makes toward achieving them. I will not expect him to stay on any schedule set by anyone who does not know him. I will provide short, structured learning sessions. I will relate every goal to something important to my child. (If I can't, perhaps he doesn't really need to learn this right now)

Notes...

Chapter
Ten

Setting
the Stage

Physical Environment

We all differ in our preferences for the type of setting in which we learn best. If our child prefers the same kind of arrangement we are comfortable with, we are fine. The difficulty comes when our learner needs a physical environment which is not comfortable for our learning or teaching style. There are several factors to be considered when developing a place to enhance learning:

Noise Level

Some people work well in a totally silent room, others need a background noise to keep themselves from hearing the growling of their stomachs, the furnace fan which goes on and off, or the traffic noises outdoors. Quiet, gentle classical music may enhance learning. A continuous sound of ocean waves, or a fan in the background may help to block out distractions. Another possibility is wearing a headset or earplugs to create silence in a roomful of sound.

Experiment to discover the noise level that is most conducive to your child's learning. Evaluate his response in many situations. If he wiggles and squirms when there is music in the background, try background noise or silence. Be willing to adjust to his need.

Lighting

Some children learn best under natural lighting, others need a bright light. Flourescent lights give some people the "blues." Others are distracted by dim lighting. Experiment and question your child. Find a lighting that works and plan to study in that kind of environment.

Temperature

Some people lose concentration and nod off if they are warm. Others cannot concentrate if they are chilled. Comfortable temperature may vary from person to person and may require adjusting clothing or thermostats.

Setting

Some need structure, clean desks in neat rows. Others learn better on the couch, or the floor. Some children truly learn better when they are standing at a table or walking around the room. Be willing to adjust if you discover your child's optimum setting is the one in which you are least comfortable.

Time of Day

Early morning, early afternoon, early evening. When do you think best? It may not be the same for your child. Some children are lethargic after eating, others cannot think by mid to late afternoon. Do not assume a child can adjust his learning needs to your desire to sleep in.

Social

Some children learn only one on one. Some do well in a group and learn from discussion and interaction with others. Some actually learn better by watching someone else do the work. Don't be hoodwinked, but do investigate without disclosing why you are experimenting!

Motivation and Persistence

Some children need frequent encouragement and continual feedback. Others are actually distracted by it and need it gathered together and given out like a package at the end of the day. Some can stick to a task unattended for hours and may actually need help transferring attention. Others need someone in the room who is listening or watching to be able to attend for more that a minute or two. Be alert and respond.

Structure

The need for structure and the ability to structure oneself varies considerably from one person to another. Age is not always the only factor. Some children may prefer to gather their materials and find a place suitable for working. Others may need you to gather all the loose ends and allow them to step into a setting already prepared to be conducive to their learning.

Food

Most of us do not think well when our stomach is growling from hunger. Children are less well able to identify this feeling or to adapt to it at the same time when they may experience it more often and more intensely than we do. On the other hand, large, heavy meals may force all the blood to the digestive system and leave little for the brain and nervous system. Be alert to signs that you are feeding too much at lunch or providing for too few snack breaks. If food is available during the work time it may benefit some while providing a distraction for others. Find a workable compromise.

Be alert to the possibility of food allergies which may affect learning. Some children react to caffeine, sugar, white flour, or milk products. Food allergies may cause befuddled thinking or hyperactivity. If you suspect this is a problem, experiment by removing what you think may be a problem and observing the results. Consult a professional. See Appendix A: Resource Guide under Allergies.

Remember, you are the adult. You have more expertise in adapting and adjusting than your child has. As he gains skill in this area, take care to adjust for his comfort when possible.

A Person,
Not a Problem!

Your child is a person, not a problem!

In former times, children were a needed segment of society! They were expected to be a contributing force in the family at a very early age - one friend of mine says from birth or before! More recently in history we have created an artificial slot in life called childhood. We have spirited children away into the halls of academia and expected them to stay put there for twelve to twenty years and suddenly "arrive" at the place where they are ready to participate in life as we know it.

This is totally unrealistic!

Children today spend ten to twenty years learning to be passive observers. At our demand they practice being submissive and compliant, waiting for someone to tell them what to do, why to do it, how to do it, and when to start and quit. They "learn" a million pieces of seemingly unrelated bits of information which someone else has determined that they need to know.

This has got to stop!

Begin looking at your child as a unique contributor. Involve him in discussions. Begin to ask his opinion. Let him make mistakes! Offer to help **when he asks** for it, and (unless he is bodily endangering himself or another) let him experiment! Let him make mistakes! He may learn best that way! Don't schedule your child's every waking hour! Let him be bored occasionally! (Boredom doesn't lead to death, but it often leads to tremendous achievements!)

Don't allow the "system" to determine what your child needs to know and when he needs to learn it! Look around the corner at who he is becoming and provide the experiences and learning opportunities he needs to get there!

Begin at the very beginning!

If your child is the most intelligent, gifted, learned person in the world, but has a terrible personality, is miserably self-centered and sees no purpose in life but the moment, have you been a successful teacher? If your child were killed in an automobile accident tomorrow and never had the opportunity to "further his education" or "make a contribution to society," could you say you were satisfied with what he knew, who he was, how you had spent your years with him?

If your child arrives at the age of twelve to fifteen knowing all the academics that have been stuffed into his head, but resenting learning, authority, and regulations, he is likely to rebel. Positive learning may stop for several years while he deals with the emotional garbage he has accumulated. He may never develop a love of learning. On the other hand, if he has learned little academically, but enjoys learning and discovery and has a good relationship with his family and friends, he is far ahead. Teach him how to use resources like the library, the encyclopedia, the Bible, an atlas, and a dictionary and he can catch up in academic knowledge within a year or two.

Begin to live as if today might be your last day ever to work with your child, for it may well be! Give your child something to live for! Involve him in life! Make your family life a place where he will want to spend his waking hours! Make your family one that will count for the future! Do something today that matters!

Notes...

Section Four

AND
FURTHERMORE

Learning in Spite of Labels

Chapter
Twelve

LEARNING
STYLES

What

boxes

define

these

children?

T here is much confusion today over the concept of learning styles. I believe that the whole concept of learning styles is an attempt to fit people into boxes in order to better understand and control them.

In reality, people cannot fit into standard boxes because God made each and every person a unique individual. Ultimately these attempts to control people must break down because God and His designs are limitless. I do feel that it is important to look at the subject because so many people are talking about it and producing materials to help you identify your teaching style and your child's learning style. I am not saying that these materials are useless. In fact, they may help you look at yourself and your child from new perspectives and give valuable hints for controlling and expanding the learning environment. I only suggest that you do not expect a magic answer that will make everything run smoothly. See Appendix A for additional resources.

I have isolated five ways of thinking about learning styles which are currently popular and seven sets of terminology for one of them! There may be some I am not aware of. Let's try to sort them out!

Personality Types

This first way of looking at learning style began before Christ! Perhaps the fact that it is such an old concept explains in part why so many ways to describe it have developed.

This way of thinking originated with Hippocrates, and was related to a theory about fluids in the blood which were supposed to affect behavior and personalities. I first heard of it through Tim LaHaye in the seventies. It is presently enjoying a resurgence of popularity. At one time, it was meant to be helpful in describing and understanding personality differences; now the emphasis seems to be on how it affects teaching and learning.

Several years ago, I took a Myers-Briggs Personality Inventory. Later, I was certified through The Institute for Motivational Living, with its DISC Profile. Then Cathy Duffy's excellent

119

treatment in her elementary Curriculum Manual caught my eye and attention. Next came *Learning Styles and Tools,* an excellent way to identify styles and organize your learning setting. I met 4 Mat through Claudia Jones' *More Parents are Teachers Too,* which briefly describes them again with new terminology. *The Family Zoo* came to my attention through Gary Smalley's video course. Each of these has a slightly different way of looking at these four types and some include combinations of the four as well.

The common thread of all of these is that there are four personality types (learning styles). They hold that by identifying an individual's learning style, you can adjust the environment to enhance learning.

The four types have been described by different people as:

Hippocrates:
Sanguine, Phlegmatic, Choleric, and Melancholy

Institute for Motivational Living:
Dominance, Influence, Steadiness, and Compliance (DISC)

Senecal (Alta Vista College):
Feeler, Thinker, Sensor, and Intuitive

Duffy:
Wiggly Willie, Competent Carl, Sociable Sue, and Perfect Paula

Golay:
Actual Spontaneous, Actual Routine, Conceptual Specific, and Conceptual Global

McCarthy (4 Mat System):
Common Sense, Dynamic, Imaginative, Analytic

Smalley (Family Zoo):
Lion, Golden Retriever, Otter, Beaver

Some of these describe the four basic styles and some describe a mixture of two types. That makes it especially difficult to converse between two different sets of terminologies.

Senses

The next way of looking at learning styles became popular in the seventies and relates to the way an individual receives information through the senses. It holds that some learners rely more heavily on one sense than another. The four main learning channels are: Visual, Auditory, Tactile (touch), and Kinesthetic (body movement). Traditional school classrooms are primarily auditory (lecture and discussion) and visual (reading) and do not provide many opportunities for those who learn best through the tactile and kinesthetic senses.

Split Brain Theory

This theory holds that each of the two hemispheres of the brain is specialized in certain ways of learning and one side is usually dominant.

Most school subjects are primarily "left brain" or sequential, verbal, and organized. Fortunately most learners also fit into this category. Left brain learning is also analytical, linguistic, logical, rational, linear, and pays attention to details.

Some children are very dominant "right brain" learners and learn best through intuition, experience, fun, and visual organization. Their way of learning may seem more like a total lack of organization! Right brain learning is more non-verbal, non-sequential, creative, and emotional. These learners see analogous relationships. They are global or see things in relation to the whole. They are skilled at synthesis. They have a poor sense of time and sequence, but a highly developed sense of space and are therefore artistic.

Multiple Intelligences

This is the newest way of looking at learning. It holds that there are seven ways of learning and that all learning will be enhanced if subjects are presented in a variety of contexts and approaches. This theory seems to be a combination of all the others.

The seven "intelligences" are:

1. **Verbal/Linguistic:** This area covers production of language and all related complexities. It involves abstract reasoning, seeing patterns, symbolic thinking, and humor. Academic areas under this heading are: reading, writing, grammar, and poetry with its metaphors and similes.

2. **Logical/Mathematical:** This area includes inductive reasoning, working with symbolic languages, and discerning relationships between pieces of information. It includes the academic learning of mathematics concepts, sequencing of events in history, and sequencing of procedures in science experiments.

3. **Visual/Spatial:** This deals with the visual arts and is based on the sense of sight and the ability to form mental pictures. Content area related to this type of learning is art with its variations of drawing, painting, sculpture, architecture, and map-making.

4. **Body/Kinesthetic:** This is the ability to express emotion and creativity through the body. These learners need hands on activities which involve touching, moving, and physically manipulating. It includes dance, gymnastics, sports, inventions, and acting.

5. **Music/Rhythmic:** This involves responding to sounds in the environment and recognition and use of rhythm and patterns of tones. It includes all aspects of music and advertising jingles.

6. **Interpersonal:** This involves communicating with people and working in group situations. It requires the ability to distinguish between moods, temperaments, intentions, and motivations. It is often highly developed in people in the service occupations of counselor, teacher, pastor and therapist.

7. Intrapersonal: This involves awareness of self and capacity for emotional response and spiritual reality.

There are other things to consider:

Birth Order

The first born child is usually more responsive to authority; he either submits or rebels forcefully. He may be more responsible and readily takes the initiative.

The second born has a greater need for acceptance and may be more competitive, gullible, loyal, impulsive, and optimistic.

The third born may adopt clownish behavior in order to get his share of the attention. Subsequent children are often influenced more by their older siblings than their parents.

Gender

Boys tend to be more aggressive, curious, and inclined to doing, touching, and taking apart.

Girls are often more compliant, verbal, and protective.

Developmental Age

All young children are kinesthetic learners, spontaneous, and need constant feedback.

Parents' Attitudes

Not all parents provide the secure, impartial, consistent atmosphere which is the best learning environment.

Personal Attitudes

Bitterness, greed, and moral impurity affect the ability to attend to learning.

Extrovert, Introvert

Shy, introverted children may learn better in a small secure and quiet setting. Outgoing children may learn better in active discussion groups.

Spiritual Gift and Calling

Holy Spirit given drives and motivations both empower and limit learning.

Environment or Stress Factors

Tension and anxiety, whether caused by the learning environment or external factors such as a death or abuse in the family, affect the ability to concentrate and learn.

I learn by talking. When I verbalize a concept, I am able to grasp it. Often concepts seem just out of reach until I am forced to verbalize. Where does that fit? I'm not sure, but there must be others who learn this way. Some counselors and psychiatrists make a fortune listening to patients solve their own problems!

I think one thing to remember about all these approaches is to thoughtfully observe, listen to, and learn from your child. He may not profit from the same type of drill which was successful for you. If he says, "I need to talk to think," or "I learn better when I'm moving," or something similar: **Listen to him!**

All of these learning styles are attempts to put children into predetermined "boxes" in order to understand and control them. God designed two boxes. Every person alive must fit into one of them. They are male and female. I believe today's society is trying to do away with these two God-given boxes while it forces people into other man-made substitutes. That is not to lessen the importance of the gifts or the calling of God. Those are paramount in our lives. But we need to be careful what labels and boxes we try to force onto children in order to control them or our concept of them.

Scripture seems more interested in the wise man and the fool, the simple and the scorner, the evil and the righteous. Don't let the latest fad control your thinking. Use it as a tool, but keep it in perspective.

Another way of looking at this is that all of these are evidence of our natural man. Our goal as Christians is to let Christ shine through us. The more we do that, the more the lines of natural personality, learning styles, and talents become fuzzy. Perhaps it is more important to identify ourselves with the nature of Christ and the gifts which are given to us by the Holy Spirit and to lead our children to do the same.

Notes...

Chapter
Thirteen

THE LAW

I don't like to even get involved in the question of law and definition and identification of "learning disabilities." I am not a lawyer and not qualified to give legal advice. I do, however, think it is imperative that you understand how the law affects you. All special needs children are eligible to receive special education and related services. Just as important, these services cannot be forced on anyone who chooses not to take advantage of them and it may be wise to defer.

The Law

Public Law (PL) 94-142, passed by Congress in 1975, defined the field of learning disabilities as a "disorder in one or more of the basic psychological processes involved in understanding or in using spoken or written language, which may manifest itself in an imperfect ability to listen, think, speak, read, write, spell, or to do mathematical calculations." It defines several areas of special education and suggests that children meeting certain guidelines be provided the "least restrictive" educational environment which is appropriate for their level of need. These statements are quite general and could include almost anyone who struggles to learn. One researcher determined that 80% of the students in America could qualify as learning disabled under this vague definition.

This law goes on to state that these problems cannot be primarily due to a lower mental functioning (low IQ), a physical disability such as blindness, deafness, or motor disability, or economic disadvantage, environmental, or cultural situations such as speaking a foreign language or not attending school because of frequent moves.

It insures that "all handicapped children have available to them a free appropriate education which includes special education and related services to meet their needs." These related services to which qualifying children (including the learning disabled) are entitled may include parent training, psychological services, residential or medical services, and after school activities.

PL 94-142 designated that an Individualized Education Plan (IEP) be made for each child receiving special education services. An IEP is a statement of the child's current functioning level, a record of how that level was determined, long term goals in any area targeted for improvement, short term objectives stated in terms of steps to reach the goals, methods and materials which will be used to implement the objectives, and a note of who is the person responsible to implement the stated goals. In a school setting the formation of the IEP is a multi-disciplinary effort. That is to say that all those involved in the child's education, from the teacher and parents to the evaluators and counselors, are to participate in determining what the goals are, who will carry them out, and how they will be taught and measured. It is a good idea for any person working with a child to set realistic goals, keep good records, and evaluate progress on a regular basis. The IEP is a way to be concise and specific in looking at the child's abilities and problems and determining the direction that his education is to take. See Chapter 19.

Section 504 of the Federal Rehabilitative Act of 1973 made compliance with the first compulsory rather than voluntary. This law mandated free and equal access for the handicapped to public buildings and education.

Public Law 99-457, passed in 1986, extended the age coverage down to age three and up to age 21. An important distinction was made for preschoolers. States are not required to label children from three to five years in order to serve them. It also established an early intervention program for infants and toddlers with disabilities. Under certain circumstances, services may be available to the family from birth of a child with physical or mental conditions expected to result in delayed learning.

Public Law 101-476, passed in 1990, amended and continued PL 94-142 and PL 99-457. The name of this act is ***Individuals with Disabilities Education Act*** or IDEA. It defines "children with disabilities" to include specific learning disabilities, speech or language impairments, and traumatic brain injury. Each of these disabilities is defined by IDEA. I am sure that in the future, PL 101-476 will be referred to more than the other older laws.

At the time of this writing, special services must be made available for children from age three to twenty-one who are identified as handicapped and to certain children from birth. Included in the term handicapped are the fields of learning disabilities, and Attention Deficit Disorder with Hyperactivity (ADHD). Children who are diagnosed as Attention Deficit Disorder but are not hyperactive (ADD) do not qualify for special services unless there is an additional handicapping condition such as learning disabilities (LD).

The problem with these labels is that there is no easy test that will clearly identify children as to having, or not having, any of these conditions. It is a judgment call based on comparison of many factors. Homeschooling families are not affected by laws regarding learning unless they have children who have been identified in the "system" as special education or are receiving services from public schools. As appealing as "free" services may appear, remember that there is always a hidden cost and that government control always accompanies government services. If you are homeschooling a special education child, you need to know about Home School Legal Defense Association (HSLDA). They make available a packet of information which answers many questions parents have and gives resources for the particular. They also provide legal defense for member families. See the Resource Guide in Appendix A for more information.

Precise and up-to-date information regarding definitions and services available may also be obtained from the *National Information Center for Children and Youth with Disabilities* (NICHCY.) This agency has a toll-free telephone and excellent free information. See Appendix A for details.

Chapter
Fourteen

Learning Problems in History

Contrary to popular opinion, the field of Learning Disabilities did not originate in the late sixties or mid seventies. There have been people in all civilizations who did not learn like others. In other societies this has been less obvious for several reasons. Previously society was less oriented toward school and academics (the hardest area for these children to find success). Adaptions in expectations and lifestyle were made automatically. Most children were educated in the home to prepare them for a career, not for another year of school. More "blue collar" jobs were available in a less technological world.

I am including some mini-biographies here both for the adults who are reading this book and for the children they have influence over. Knowing that others have struggled against apparently unsurmountable odds in their childhood and youth, yet risen to the top in some field, may be encouraging both to the parent who is discouraged and to the child who thinks he'll never amount to anything. I do not necessarily endorse these people or their lifestyles, but note that they have overcome difficult odds to climb to success. They may or may not have been diagnosed as learning disabled, but they all struggled against various learning problems.

You will discover that many of these successful people were educated at home. Some of them were utter failures at school. If they had been forced to remain in that unproductive (for them) environment, many of them might have had far different lives. School is only one part of life. It is temporary. Failure or success in that specific environment is not related in any way to a person's worth or ability to succeed in other environments. Indeed at times the very ones who are difficult to teach and lead, when mature, may be the leaders and teachers of their own generation. Leaders find it difficult to follow even when they are young. At times it is the very struggle against difficult odds that cause a person to develop the skills and maturity necessary to deal with life successfully.

Hans Christian Anderson did not study or do well in school. Tall and skinny, he was the brunt of many jokes and much teasing. His mother couldn't read or write, but his father read to him. After his father's death when he was eleven, he stayed home and made up stories. The story of the Ugly Duckling is probably his autobiography. Children of every era have been delighted with his fairy tales.

Michael Faraday, called the *Father of Electronics*, had a speech impediment which brought ridicule from classmates and teachers. His mother took him out of school and he worked to improve his speech and discover the hidden laws of God. His world renowned discoveries in the field of science brought him an honorary Doctor of Civil Law degree from Oxford University. Many dignitaries including England's royal family attended his science lectures.

President Woodrow Wilson was nine before he mastered the alphabet and did not learn to read until he was eleven. His parents were quite defensive in public, but his father encouraged deep thinking about religion and politics and taught him at home in early years. Determined, he struggled to learn, and on his own developed a strong power of concentration and a nearly photographic memory.

Nelson Rockefeller had a severe reading problem. This didn't stop him from becoming Vice President of the United States and governor of New York.

Thomas Edison's formal education lasted only three months. Then his teacher called him "addled" which means retarded. His mother withdrew him from school, took him home and made a game of "exploring" the exciting world of knowledge. He was deaf from age 12, but he didn't mind because he found it easier to concentrate. His record of over a thousand patents includes the movie projector, the microphone, the record player, and the electric light bulb.

Albert Einstein, the mathematics genius, was slow learning to talk and thought to be retarded even by his parents. He was a stubborn student who rebelled against unthinking memorization which was demanded by his school. Later, he realized that it was because he wasn't aware of time and space as a youngster that he didn't take them for granted. When he finally noticed these concepts, he had the maturity to think about them in a different way. He was fascinated with a magnetic compass given to him during a childhood illness and determined to better understand the forces behind its functions.

Albert Schweitzer was tiny and weak at birth and no one thought he would survive. He was a dreamer and had trouble paying attention in school, yet went on to be a famous missionary doctor in the African jungle.

Ann Bancroft had trouble learning to read and was held back in school, yet she was the first woman to reach the North Pole. She traveled with the Will Steger expedition in 1976.

Gallileo Galilei seemed uninterested in working hard, making money, or studying what his parents asked. Though blind in later years, he made many contributions to our understanding of mathematics, science, and astronomy.

John Audubon, the great bird painter, failed at everything he should have been studying in school when he was young. He was out watching birds. His parents then sent him to a boarding school where he excelled in studying nature.

Helen Keller was left blind and deaf by a serious illness when she was two years old. Due to a dedicated teacher, she learned to read and write and eventually to speak. She graduated with honors from Radcliffe College and went on to improve the conditions for the blind throughout the world. The books she authored have been translated into more than fifty languages.

George Washington Carver, barely survived at birth. He grew up to be thin and puny and had a squeaky voice with a stutter. He was ten years old before he talked so people could understand him. Determined to go to school when it was forbidden for slaves or Negroes, he walked a long distance to go to high school. He finished his education, and became a famous scientist who discovered many uses for peanuts and found a way to make plastic from soybeans.

Greg Louganis became an Olympic gold medal winner though he had speech and reading problems in school.

Bruce Jenner had severe reading problems, but went on to win an Olympic gold medal.

Susan Hampshire had trouble paying attention in school, but won three Emmy Awards for acting on television.

Ben Carson, climbed from the bottom of his class to become an honor student by reading two books a week and writing book reports for his mother who couldn't even read them. He is now a world famous pediatric neurosurgeon.

Joy Ridderhoff, was an absent-minded student who went on to become missionary to many nations. She founded Gospel Recordings to give the Scriptures to people in their native language.

Chuck Yeager was described by one of his teachers as quite ordinary and a bit "slow," but his mother instilled in him the importance of personal responsibility. He became a fighter pilot and was the first person to fly an aircraft faster than the speed of sound.

Jim Thorpe, a Sauk and Fox Indian from Oklahoma, was never a good student and had trouble fitting in. He preferred to be free to hunt and fish and frequently ran away even though he returned to face a beating. He won two Olympic gold metals in the difficult sport events of the decathon and the pentathlon, and then went on to become a football star.

Chris Burke had Down syndrome and his parents were told to put him in an institution at birth. Instead, they took him home and surrounded him with love. He said it was like having five teachers since both parents and three siblings showered him with attention. He didn't speak until he was eighteen months old or walk until he was two. When he saw another boy with Down syndrome on television, he contacted him and began a friendship. He has starred in the television show, *Life Goes On*.

Kristi Yamaguchi was born with turned in legs. She had casts put on when she was only two weeks old. They were changed every two weeks until her first birthday. She wore corrective shoes connected with a bar until she was four. Her parents started her skating to improve and strengthen her legs. She went on to win two world championships in women's skating and an Olympic gold medal.

Michelle Smithdas was totally deaf by the age of sixteen and blinded in a snowmobiling accident at the age of twenty-one. Assisted by a volunteer from the Helen Keller National Center for Deaf-Blind Youth and Adults, she earned a master's degree in education and now is an instructor at the center.

Fill in the blanks with details about your own child!

When _____ was

_____ years old, it was very difficult for (him/her)_____ to

_____

(He/She) _____ had already struggled hard to learn to _____.

_____

(He/She) _____ had learned the hard way that it is very

important to _____.

(He/She) _____ continues to have problems with things like

_____ _____, but is very good at _____.

(His/Her) _____ plans for the future include _____

_____ and

_____.

We are sure *(he/she)*_____ will succeed because *(he/she)*_____

_____

(He/She) _____ is especially grateful that _____helped

(him/her _____ to _____

_____

You also need to know that _____

_____

_____

_____

_____

_____

_____

_____

_____

Notes...

Chapter
Fifteen

HISTORY
REPEATED

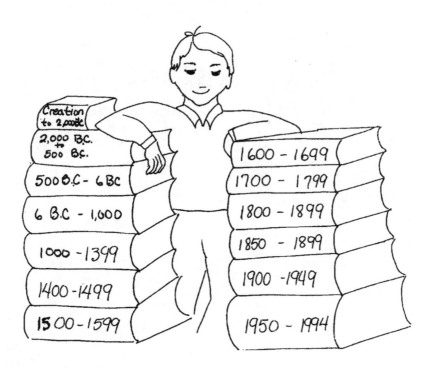

"Those who do not remember the past
are condemned to repeat it."
— George Santayana
The Life of Reason

"My people are destroyed
through lack of knowledge."
— Hosea 4:6

Martin Luther (1483-1546) said: "I am much afraid that schools will prove to be great gates of hell, unless they diligently labor in explaining the Holy Scriptures, and engraving them on the hearts of youth."

William Penn, in *"Frame of Government,"* wrote: "That all persons...having children...shall cause such to be instructed in reading and writing, so that they may be able to read the Scriptures and to write by the time they attain to 12 years of age."

The first law regarding education in the United States of America was the **Old Deluder Satan Act** of Connecticut and Massachusetts of 1642. It was written by the people who had come to America because of such civil atrocities as the Inquisition and the Crusades, most of which happened in the name of Christianity. They believed the cause of these atrocities was that the average person did not have access to the Word of God and the ability to read it in his own language. The Old Deluder Satan Act says: "Being the one chief project that old deluder, Satan, to keep men from the knowledge of the scriptures..."

106 of the first 108 colleges in this country were founded on Christianity. Following are quotes from the writings of three of them:

Harvard, founded in 1636, "Let every student be plainly instructed and consider well the main end of his life and studies is to know God and Jesus Christ and therefore to lay Christ in the bottom as the only foundation of all sound knowledge and learning. Everyone shall so excercise himself in reading the Scriptures twice a day that he shall be ready to give an account of his proficiency therein both in theoretical observations of languages and logic, and in practical and spiritual truths." 52% of the early graduates of Harvard became pastors!

Yale, founded in 1701 for liberal education: "Seeing God is the giver of all wisdom, every scholar, besides private or secret prayer shall be present morning and evening at public prayer."

Princeton, the "Johnny come lately" of the early universities and founded in 1746, educated 87 of our founding fathers with these words: "Cursed be all learning that is contrary to the cross of Christ."

President of Princeton, **John Witherspoon** was also a patriot, a signer of the constitution, and a member of congress. His works, published after his death, said this: "What follows from this? That he is the best friend to American liberty who is most sincere and active in promoting true and undefiled religion and who sets himself with the greatest firmness to bear down profanity and immorality of every kind. Whoever is an avowed enemy of God, I scruple not to call him an enemy of his country."

Benjamin Rush, another signer of the Declaration of Independence, a physician, the surgeon and founder of Pennsylvania Hospital, wrote a paper titeled, *A Defense of the Use of the Bible in Schools: a letter from Dr. Benjamin Rush.* In it he says: "Dear Sir, it is now several months since I promised to give you my reasons for preferring the Bible, as a schoolbook, to all other compositions. Before I state my arguments, I shall assume the five following propositions:

1. That Christianity is the only true and perfect religion and that in proportion as mankind adopt and obey its precepts, they will be wise and happy.

2. That a better knowledge of this religion is to be acquired by reading the Bible, than in any other way.

3. That the Bible contains more knowledge necessary to man in his present state, than any other book in the world.

4. That knowledge is most durable, and religious instruction most useful, when imparted early in life.

5. That the Bible, when not read in schools, is seldom read in any subsequent period of life.

My arguments in favor of the use of the Bible as a schoolbook are founded:

1. In the constitution of the human mind, the memory is the first facility which opened in the minds of children. Of how much consequence, then, must it be, to impress it with the great truth of subjects.

2. There is a peculiar aptitude in the minds of children for religious knowledge. I have constantly found them, in the first six or seven years of their lives, more inquisitive upon religious subjects than upon any others."

Dr. Jedediah Morse, father of American geography, wrote a book called *Geography Made Easy* in 1784. In it he said: "To the kindly influence of Christianity we owe that degree of civil freedom and political and social happiness which mankind now enjoys. In proportion as the genuine effects of Christianity are diminished in any nation, in the same proportion will the people of that nation recede from the blessings of genuine freedom. I hold this to be a truth confirmed by experience (and) it follows that all efforts made to destroy the foundations of our holy religion ultimately tend to the subversion also of our political freedom and happiness. Whenever the pillars of Christianity shall be overthrown, our present republican forms of government, and all the blessings which flow from them, must fall with them."

George Washington, our first President from 1789 to 1797, said: "He who thinks morality can be maintained without religion is seriously mistaken. Reason and experience both forbid us to expect that national morality can prevail in exclusion of religious principle." The Indians highly respected him and several of them brought their youth to Washington to be educated in American schools. In a speech given May 12, 1779, Mr. Washington said to them, "You do well to wish to learn (in our schools) our arts and way of life, and above all the religion of Jesus Christ. These will make you a greater and happier people than you are. Congress will do everything they can to assist you in this wise intention."

Thomas Jefferson, as president of the schoolboard for the Washington, D.C. schools while he was also President of the

United States, wrote the plan of education for the schools of the capital of the United States. The Bible and Watt's hymnal (which was full of doctrine) were the primary reading texts. He also remarked, "I have always said and always will say that the studious perusal of the sacred volume will make us better citizens."

Noah Webster in *The History of the United States,* wrote: "It is the sincere desire of this writer that our citizens should early understand that the genuine source of correct republican principles is the Bible, particularly the New Testament, or the Christian religion."

In another book, *Advice for Youth,* Noah Webster wrote: "The moral principles and precepts contained in the Scriptures ought to form the basis of all our civil constitutions and laws...all the miseries and evils which men suffer from (vice, crime, ambition, injustice, oppression, slavery, and war) proceed from their despising and neglecting the precepts contained in the Bible." From the same book come these words. "The religion which has introduced civil liberty is the religion of Christ and his apostles. This is genuine Christianity; to this we owe our free constitutions of government." After his death an epitaph was written in his Blue Backed Speller which stated that he taught millions to read, but not one to sin.

The **Northwest Ordinance** was signed into law in 1789 by President Washington to enumerate the requirements for statehood in the United States of America. Article 3 of the Ordinance provides that in order to become a state, there must be schools which teach religion, morality, and knowledge. During that same year, the first amendment was written, not to separate church and state, but to preclude the establishment of a state church. All the states joining the union after 1789 had to establish schools which would teach religion (assumed to be Christianity) and morality, as well as knowledge.

Daniel Webster, born in 1782 during the American Revolution, listened to all the founding fathers in his formative years. Almost a permanent fixture in the Senate, he was also a formidable lawyer and well-known orator. When a Philadelphia school, headed by Steven Girard who was a student of the French Enlightenment, decided to teach morality without religion, the case was taken to the Supreme Court. Daniel Webster opposed the school. The argument lasted three days in court. Webster wrote this version of what happened:

"There is an authority still more imposing and awful. When little children were brought into the presence of the Son of God, his disciples proposed to send them away; but he said, 'Suffer the little children to come unto Me!' Unto me; he did not send them first for lessons in morals to the schools of the Pharisees or to the unbelieving Sadducees, nor to read the precepts and lessons phylacteries on the garments of the Jewish priesthood; he said nothing of different creeds or clashing doctrines; but he opened at once to the youthful mind, the everlasting fountain of living waters, the only source of eternal truths: 'Suffer the little children to come unto Me!' And that injunction is of perpetual obligation. It addresses itself today with the same earnestness and the same authority which attended its utterance to the Christian world. It is of force everywhere, and at all times. It extends to the ends of the earth, it will reach to the end of time, always and everywhere sounding in the ears of men, with an emphasis which no repetition can weaken, and with an authority which nothing can supersede; 'Suffer the little children to come unto Me' and not only my heart, and my judgment, my belief, and my conscience instruct me that this great precept should be obeyed, but the idea is such that the solemn thoughts connected with it so crowd upon me, it is so utterly at variance with its system of philosophical morality which we have heard advocated, that I stand and speak here in fear of being influenced by my feelings to exceed the proper line of my professional duty. Go thy way at this time, is the language of philosophical morality, and I will send for thee at a more convenient season. This is the language of Mr. Girard in his will. In this there is neither religion nor reason".

— From the *Works of Daniel Webster*
which he himself edited before his death.

In this case the court ruled that we will not have a school in America that will not teach Christian principles. Part of its statement reads: "Why may not the Bible, and especially the New Testament, be read and taught as a divine revelation in the schools?" "It's general precepts expounded, and its glorious principles of morality inculcated? Where can the purest principles of morality be learned so clearly or so perfectly as from the New Testament?"

John Quincy Adams, President from 1825 to 1829, said the first and almost the "only book deserving of universal attention is the Bible."

William McGuffey, the schoolmaster of the nation, in the 1837 *Eclectic Third Reader,* wrote "The design of the Bible is evidently to give us correct information concerning the creation of all things...The Scriptures are especially designed to make us wise unto salvation through faith in Christ Jesus, to reveal to us the mercy of the Lord in him, to form our minds after the likeness of God our Savior; to build up our souls in wisdom and faith, in love and holiness; to make us thoroughly furnished unto good works, enabling us to glorify God on earth; and to lead us to an imperishable inheritance among the spirits of just men made perfect, and finally to be glorified with Christ in heaven..."

Abraham Lincoln, President from 1861 to 1865, said, "All the good from the Savior of the world is communicated through this book (the Bible). But for the book we could not know right from wrong. All the things desirable to men are contained in it." He also said, "The philosophy of the school room in one generation will be the philosophy of government in the next."

On March 3, 1865 an **Act of Congress** added the phrase "In God We Trust" to our coins.

In 1892 the **Teachers' Union**, in celebration of the 400th anniversary of Christopher Columbus landing in America, wrote down the Legacy of Education. They noted that elementary education which had been started in this country by the church, had since been voluntarily relinquished to the state, and said: "If the study of the Bible is to be excluded from all state schools, if the inculcation of the principles of Christianity is to have no place in the daily program, if the worship of God is to form no part of the general exercise of these public elementary schools, then the good of the state would be better served by restoring all schools to church control."

Supreme Court Justice **David J. Brewer**, who served from 1890 to 1910, gave a lecture titled *The United States a Christian Nation*. It said, in part, "This Republic is classified among the Christian nations of the world. It was so formally declared by the Supreme Court of the United States in the case of *Holy Trinity Church vs. United States 143 U.S. 47.*"

Woodrow Wilson, President from 1913 to 1921, is quoted, "The Bible is the only supreme source of a revelation of the meaning of life, the nature of God, and the spiritual meaning of men. It is the only guide of life that really leads the spirit in the way of peace and of salvation."

Calvin Coolidge, President from 1925 to 1929, said: "The foundations of our society and our government rests so much on the teachings of the Bible that it would be difficult to support them if faith in these teachings would cease to be."

The doorway to the inner courtroom of the **Supreme Court Building**, built in 1935, is engraved with the ten "Commandments of Almighty God."

In 1963 **William Earnest Smith** wrote "About the McGuffeys." 125 million copies of McGuffey had been sold already. He wrote that "Except the Bible, no other book or set of books has influenced the American mind so much."

Since **prayer and the Bible** were removed from the public schools in the 1960's, divorce rates are up 100%. Pregnancies to girls 10-14 are up 500%. Sexually transmitted diseases have risen 200%. America now leads the world in violent crime, divorce, teenage pregnancies, voluntary abortions, and illegal drugs.

Attention Deficit Disorder ADD, ADHD

Attention Deficit Disorder,
Attention Deficit Hyperactive Disorder,
Hyperactive, Hyperkinetic

Many parents are searching for answers in a field that is filled with controversy and confusion. Experts vary greatly on the need for a definition of the problem currently called ADD/ADHD (Attention Deficit Disorder/ Attention Deficit Hyperactivity Disorder) and on treatment of the symptoms of "excess energy, impulsivity and inattention." No matter what you think, you will find some expert who agrees with you. You need to be aware first of all, that until recently there was no such term, no "doctors" certified for treating it, no special funds to assist schools in handling children with it, and no one writing about it. Once it was "identified" (or defined), it mushroomed almost as fast as the first atomic bomb. One must wonder why it was needed in the first place, and why it has grown so fast in the second place. More children are being diagnosed with this problem than ever before. I think there are many reasons:

- I think there actually are more problems than previously because of changes in our society. This includes early, continuous, and excessive exposure to television and video games. These teach a child to have a very short - usually ten second - attention span, and teach him at the same time that he cannot change his environment, has no responsibility for it, and there is no morality in the choices he makes. In addition, the time a child gives to these activities is stolen from other activities which would better develop visual, perceptual, visual-motor, and attention skills. The diet of the average American child is overloaded with empty calories, chemicals, and additives of all kinds and his body is the result of several generations of the same. Discipline both at home and in schools is often inconsistent, poorly approached, or absent altogether. Training is unknown and often harsh discipline is substituted. Children are seldom included naturally in full time family activities. Structured games (board games, table games, charades, etc.) and imaginative play seem to be a thing of the past. All these things add to create children who haven't learned sustained attention, patience, perseverance, and calm consistent approach to problem solving.

- I also believe that this and other labels are being used indiscriminately to increase funds for educational programs, to justify lack of discipline, to pacify parents, to justify medication which may keep the child subdued, and to explain away teacher's inability to educate or even control children in the large group settings which classrooms demand.

- Formal, paper-and-pencil, force-fed education is being started younger and younger. Children aren't developmentally ready and they miss out on the activities they truly need to develop vision, perceptual-motor and other school-related skills.

- Parents and educators are following educational programs and formula patterns without any clear convictions as to why they are using what they are using. Programs and approaches are started and abandoned. Some children do not respond well to this type of inconsistency.

The child who struggles with ADD/ADHD is poor at focusing his attention. He may dash from one thing to another because he hears and sees everything or he may never seem to get involved with anything. He is poor at blocking out the variety of stimuli in his environment. He hears the curtains rustle, sees the dust flecks floating, feels the breeze lift the hairs off his arms. He has difficulty shutting out these other things which stimulate his body and brain in order to concentrate only on what you are saying.

Even more than the average child, children who have problems directing their attention need love, training, consistent expectations, discipline and rewards for appropriate behavior. They need consistent, structured settings for learning. They do not handle well loosely structured situations (noisy restaurants and cafeterias, recess, parties, moving from one activity to another etc.). It is important that they know what is expected, what will be rewarded and what will be disciplined. They need appropriate outlets for their excess energy, but often do not succeed in group activities. They therefore need individual opportunities like swimming, biking, roller blading, and so on. When they must remain quiet and/or still for a length of time, they need something to "fiddle" with (sports exercise putty, a balloon filled with flour, construction toys like Legos™, blank paper and colored pencils, etc.). (It is just as important that these materials be used in this situation as tools and not thrown or used in other inappropriate ways.) They need to see progress (charts, lists to check off, small assignments done, etc.). They need to be rewarded (verbally, with hugs, pleased looks, etc.) for appropriate behavior and achievements. If they get more attention for being naughty than for being good, guess which they'll choose to continue. They need opportunities to increase their attention span (auditory, visual, and task focus) in tiny increments. They need to know their limits and be held to them firmly but lovingly. They need to be taught that they are just as responsible for their behavior as any other person, but may need to work harder to receive the same results. They also need to know that their energy is a great gift of God which, like all His gifts, must be channeled to be effective.

Here are some things you can do to help your child.

1. **Love and enjoy your child.** This is most important of all. Look for times and ways to enjoy your child and your relationship with him. Find situations which you can enjoy together. Spend time with him doing what he likes to do. Let him join you in doing what you like to do. He won't find

acceptance in many places or from many people and it is **essential** that he knows that you love him (always) and enjoy him (at least some times!)

2. **This child needs to know what is expected** even more than the average child. It is important to have as few rules as possible. The rules you do have need to be stated very precisely and in a positive manner. "Our family respects the needs and feelings of others." He also needs to know what will happen if he breaks the rules. "Each time you are disrespectful, your evening bedtime will be moved forward ten minutes." Then that needs to be followed through. If he finds he can whine or pout and change your mind, you are in for a lot of whining and pouting! He will test the limits, but if you are consistent and firm, you will all win in the end.

3. **He needs consistent discipline.** If he is punished one day for what was ignored the day before, the mixed signals are confusing and lead to insecurity and volatile emotions. Likewise, problems are created if Mom allows what Dad punishes, or just the opposite. Don't have more rules than both Mom and Dad are willing to enforce.Firm but gentle must be the order of the day. You must know what you expect, know what the limits are, and communicate them to him in a way that he understands. You cannot allow him to break the rule until you are angry and then yell and strike out. **He must be stopped early in disobedience and redirected.**

4. **When a transition is necessary, he needs a warning** and he needs to have some control over the situation. "Johnny, in fifteen minutes we need to leave to go grocery shopping. Would you like to clean up now and get a book to read in the car, or would you like to play a few minutes longer and let me choose the book?" With a statement like that, you gain his cooperation. He knows what will happen. He understands that he will have to stop what he is doing.

153

He feels in control because he is offered a specific, controlled choice. Avoid telling him at the last second, "Come on. Right now. Just stop what you are doing and come with me. We're already late." That approach is confrontive and disruptive and sure to get results – unfortunate results like stress, fights, and tension.

5. **Don't require that he sit still while he listens.** Give him something for his hands and/or mouth to be doing during learning and listening times. Both sitting still and listening require his full attention. If his hands have something to do, like drawing, playing with construction toys, or squeezing bread dough, he will be better able to listen. If his mouth is busy with candy or gum (all right, use the sugarless kind), his ears are free to listen. When it is necessary for him to sit still, as in a doctor's office or car, provide hand-held video games, drawing supplies, or a book he wants to read. If he is in church, firmly rub his back.

6. **Practice paying attention.** Make a game of learning to sit still. Set a timer for one minute. Challenge him to sit very still moving only his eyes until the timer rings. If he succeeds, praise and reward him. If he doesn't, try 45 seconds, or thirty seconds. Do that for three days in a row, and then increase the time by half. When that is easy, don't increase the time, but add a distraction. Talk to him, sing, or move around the room. Reward him for ignoring you and sitting still. Clap your hands together, jump up and down, or make silly faces. When he can still sit still for 90 seconds and ignore your deliberate distractions, gradually increase the amount of time you expect him to sit still and continue with the distractions.

7. **Don't overload his senses!** He is easily over-stimulated. When he has a bad reaction, note where he is and what was distracting or provoking. Unstructured events, large numbers of people, loud concerts, many things going on at once, and new situations may create problems. Plan to avoid these

situations as much as possible. When this can't be done, limit the amount of time he is there, and watch closely for overload. At the first sign, find a way to get him away and don't allow the situation to escalate.

8. **Find outlets for his energy.** Gymnastics, swimming, and other individual sports give vent for his energy without putting him in potentially explosive situations. Help him understand that his energy is a wonderful asset which needs to be channeled. **His energy will be a tremendous blessing to him as an adult if he learns how to handle it!** Teach him early to jog, run, swim, and play ball and allow those activities as breaks between academics as often as possible. A five-minute controlled run or other exercise every 30 to 60 minutes in the midst of academics helps tremendously. A mini-tramp in the classroom to be used for breaks or rewards may be a lifesaver!

9. **Use a teaching style which allows him to get totally involved** in a controlled way. This means body, mind, and spirit, not just see, say, and write. He will learn best when he can interact with the information; plant seeds, build a fort, take apart an appliance, and so on. Start with two minutes of concentration followed by three minutes of controlled physical activity. (If he can't concentrate for at least two minutes, he is not ready for this type of activity. Go back to teaching attention #6.) Work toward twenty minutes of concentration followed by two minutes of physical break.

10. **Separate behavior from the person.** A child who struggles with impulse and attention control needs to know that he is responsible for his behavior, but he is not his behavior. Assure him that, while his behavior is not always acceptable, he is still loved, approved of and appreciated. "That behavior will not be tolerated. You are always welcome, but that behavior is not. Go to your bedroom (or a time out area, or we will leave the restaurant, or whatever) until that behav-

ior is under control." "I love you so much, but that behavior is (dangerous, distracting all the people, displeasing to God, etc.). We will have to leave (if you persist, or until that is under control." "I **always** love you, but I like you better when you're not behaving this way," is valid. Help him take control of his behavior. **Teach appropriate behavior.** Assist him in any way he needs to do what is right and appropriate. When his behavior is inappropriate, remove him from the situation and redirect his attention and energy into appropriate channels. Encourage him to own his behavior and discuss how he might have handled it differently. Give him the tools to evaluate his behavior and encourage him to make good choices. Teach godly reasons for choosing appropriate behavior (See NATHHAN News article in resource section.)

11. **Include him in decision making whenever possible.** Don't give options: (Are you ready? Do you want to? Would you like to?) unless he **really** has an option. When there is no decision, or you have already made it, don't offer a choice! This child needs to grow up and be involved in decisions about his learning as young as possible. He will succeed **only** with a great amount of effort on his own part, and will be willing to put that forth only if he sees it as worth it all. "Yes, it is harder for you to (listen, concentrate, sit still, etc.), but it is very important that you learn to (whatever). I will help you as much as possible, but you will have to work very hard to remember (that it is important, that it is necessary, and that right now all other things have to be ignored, etc.). We will work together. Now let's see you (listen for five minutes, etc.). As often as possible, he needs to understand the purpose of what he is doing and be motivated by his own agreement that it is important. When he must do what you say, when you say, be firm and controlled and assist him in being obedient.

12. **Give him things to do that he can accomplish and take pride in!** It will be very tricky to keep this child from feeling worthless and inadequate. Praise him every **real** chance you get - not just for his achievement but for: who he is, that he is, just being, or trying. Believe in him and in <u>his potential to become a person that you will both like</u>. Find something he is really interested in (motorcycles, helicopters, horses, etc.) and try to associate anything you want him to learn with what he likes. Independently, he will rarely see a project through to completion. Give him some very simple projects (one at a time!!) and see that they are finished (even if you have to assist him). Then help him identify and enjoy the good feeling that comes from having finished the job.

13. **Discover strengths and encourage their expression.** These children are usually very loving, giving, and sensitive to the underdog. They may be excellent artists. They are often quite skilled with taking things apart and sometimes can even get them back together! Provide raw materials and time for them to explore their talents. Give them some broken appliances and tools and a corner in a basement or garage. If he takes something apart and can't get it back together, he has the raw materials for a new invention.

14. **Allow him to make mistakes as long as he is not endangering himself or someone else.** Don't worry if he tries to glue crayon shavings on paper or tape metal pieces together. He'll figure out that it won't work and try something else. He'll be less discouraged by his own mistakes if he is allowed to explore what works without constant criticism or advice.

15. **Assist him in organizing his time, possessions, and tools.** He is not likely to be a natural organizer and will need more specific instructions more often to a later age than most children. If you want him to clean his room, organize it

157

with him telling him why you keep things where you do. When it is done, photograph each small section - each wall, dresser drawers and tops, closet, and so on. Post the photographs inside the closet and help him refer to them when you clean it together next time. Before school starts each day, organize his desk and make sure there is an adequate supply of sharpened pencils, paper, etc. Before he leaves the house make sure he has a backpack filled with whatever he will need while he is gone. Weekly spend time together organizing his work area and tools. This **is** part of school and essential if he is to become a successful adult! It is important that you do not pile one assignment upon another and then expect him to finish them all before a certain time. Each task must be given full attention for a specified time or until completed. He is not likely to be able to organize his time or his possessions and needs your assistance to do so.

16. **Make sure he has at least one good friend outside the family.** This may be an older child who is in on the plan, an adult, or even a pet. Be sure this person is encouraging and positive. Your child needs to have affirmation from someone other than Mom and Dad.

How can I help him listen?

- Allow him to hold and mold clay or silly putty as he listens.

- Save gum or hard candy as something he gets only when it is time to listen.

- Allow him to use crayons, markers, etc. with blank paper as he listens.

- As you read him a story, or in church, firmly rub his back.

How can I help him slow down?

- Decrease the stimulus in his learning environment.

- Only ask for slow down when it is essential.

- Structure his learning time and always include something for his hands and/or mouth to be doing.

- He, above all children, needs to know what is expected, needs consistent discipline.

- Allow some kind of white background noise (fan, air conditioner, sound of ocean waves, very gentle and quiet classical music, even quiet static) when he is to concentrate.

- Start with very small times of concentration interspersed with longer periods of total body involvement such as running, stretching, or somersaults. Gradually increase concentration time.

- Keep him out of situations that you know will over-stimulate him. (Unstructured situations, large numbers of people, loud concerts, etc.).

A timer is the best tool I have found to assist children who struggle to maintain attention. Be sure to purchase a silent one, as the "tick-tick" can only add to the child's difficulty. The timer may be used to limit struggle. If you know that math is difficult, for instance, ask the child to work hard for (five, ten, fifteen at the most) minutes. If he does this, reward him with a two-minute break to get a drink, jump on a mini-tramp, do five somersaults or jumping jacks or do something which uses energy and doesn't demand attention. Then try it again for ten minutes, followed by a short break. Use the timer to signal the end of the break as well as the end of the time for attention. Use the timer with any assignment. First you need to know how long the child needs to perform the expected task. Set the timer for longer than he needs, for example if he needs fifteen minutes, set the timer for 25 minutes. If he finishes (work completed and well done) before the timer goes off, he may have a break until the timer signals the end. If he doesn't finish, change to another type of task and return to the unfinished work later. Have him concentrate for a designated period of time (increasing from seconds to twenty minutes). When the timer signals, he may take a designated time (decreasing from one minute to ten seconds) to break the concentration. At first he will need a signal to get back to work as well. The timer's signal should be gentle and unobtrusive, but definite.

When you make your family's rules, it is important that both parents agree. It is equally important that you have no more rules than you are both willing and able to enforce. I have narrowed necessary rules down to three:

- Children, obey your parents. This is the only biblical mandate for children.

- Do what you say you'll do. This is one of two rules agreed upon by all known societies.

- Don't hurt anyone. This is the other rule agreed upon by all known societies.

- Choose to love. Love God. Love others. Love yourself.

You may think that these suggestions are good for all children. That is true. Children with ADD/ADHD are children first. They will need somewhat tighter and stronger structure and more encouragement to develop the inner controls which come so hard for them. They will need more help controlling themselves until they do develop inner control. It is a mistake to excuse their behavior and allow them to run wild. That leads to less control and more wildness. They need **controlled** opportunity to release their energy and **structured** assistance to make good decisions for a longer period than other children.

You will need additional resources. There are many on the

160

market. They offer conflictive and sometimes destructive advice. You can find experts who agree with you whatever you believe. Check out the experts' experience and background before you believe everything you read!

Notes...

Vision Skills
Development

Thee are several reasons why I have included this section. It has been my experience over the years that a large percentage of my learning disabled students have had visual perceptual and/or visual skills deficits. Early in my career, I worked with an optometrist who specialized in children's vision problems. We accidentally discovered that I was repressing vision in one eye. After a few months of training, I got off high risk car insurance! I had had a wreck every time I drove an unfamiliar car because I had no depth perception. I became very sensitive to little symptoms that children were struggling with poor eye function. (These can have **nothing** to do with vision acuity that is commonly the only thing measured when you get your eyes examined.) (See "physical exam," on page 50).

Become quietly observant of your child. When he does close up work, does he:

- Hold the paper too close or at an odd angle?
- Tilt his head or contort his body?
- Let his hair hang over one eye?
- Rub his eyesore squint or blink frequently?
- Reread, lose his place, or skip lines?
- Contort his face or grind his teeth?
- Hide one eye behind a hand?
- Stop frequently to look away and back again?
- Sit at an odd angle?
- Have difficulty copying?
- Have more problems the longer he reads?
- Hold an arm or wrist between one eye and his work?
- Complain of words jumping or disappearing?
- Push up one cheek so that eye can't see?
- Hold the paper too far from his head?
- Twist and wiggle continually?
- Daydream?
- Show inconsistency (knows a word, but not when it is repeated on the next line or page)?

These may be signs that he is not using his eyes efficiently. If he hasn't developed these skills naturally by age six or seven, he may need help. These skills can be trained. He will not outgrow this. (Remember my high risk car insurance?) Not every optometrist has received the specialized training necessary to diagnose or treat these children's vision problems. Opthamologists are trained in disease of the eye, but they do not deal with these other functions, which they call central processing problems.

Before your child reaches kindergarten age, he should be examined by a professional trained to evaluate near-space visual skills including, but not limited to visual tracking, accomodation, fusion, focus far to near, eye movement control, and sustaining clear focus.

Some good habits for healthy vision:

- Proper work distance (from eye to paper or book) is the Harmon distance, or the distance from the elbow to the first knuckle. Less or more is harmful to vision.

- Have adequate and proper lighting.

- Use a slant board for writing. Try to make the angle of the work surface parallel to the plane of the face.

- Take frequent vision breaks. Especially during close-up work, frequently look away at something in the distance.

- Involve the child in a variety of visual tasks daily. Don't have all tasks involve close-up vision. Have him read, run, write, play ball, draw, play with toys. Vary the demands on his eyes through the day.

There are ways to help your child at home.

There are optometrists who specialize
in children's vision problems.

**For Resources for Vision Development
see Appendix A**

Notes...

Speech and Language Development

I have run into so many homeschooling families who are uncertain what normal development is that I decided to cover this topic briefly.

Normal Development of Language Skills

AGE OF DEVELOPMENT	LANGUAGE SKILL
early months	babbling
6-12 months	nonsense words
12 months and later	1 word utterances
2 years and later	2 word utterances
3 years and later	beginning grammar
7 to 8 years	adult competence

In each of these if a child is more than a year late, you may need to see a professional for evaluation. During the nonsense word stage from six to twelve months, it is essential that the child have auditory feedback. If he is deaf and does not hear the responses, he will not develop language naturally. Provide a mirror for him to watch his own speech movements, allow him to see the person who is speaking, and allow him to alternately feel your throat and his own as you make sounds. If the parents of a hearing child are deaf and non-speaking, they need to see that he spends significant time with speaking adults during language development stages.

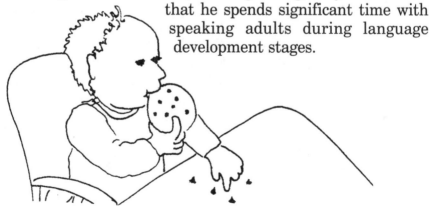

Normal Development of Speech Sounds

AGE AT DEVELOPMENT	SPEECH SOUNDS
3 1/2 years	p, b, m, w, h
4 1/2 years	t, d, n, k, g, ng, y
5 1/2 years	f, ch
6 1/2	z, zh, l, j, th (voiceless)
7 1/2	r, s, z, th (voiced)

These are normal development times. If your child is struggling with some of these sounds long after the "normal development time," you may want to consult a professional.

Straight Talk, by Maria Lapish is a program to enable parents to work on speech development at home. With this program you can intervene earlier in a warm home environment. (See Appendix A for information.)

Stuttering

Remain calm and accepting. Do not call the child's attention to the potential problem. Model correct speech. Provide a warm, calm atmosphere. Encourage talking in comfortable cheerful settings. Do not demand speech in tense or hurried situations. Do everything in your power to make speech a pleasant experience. Tell and read a loud stories. Tell jokes and make opportunities to sing together. Assure him if he asks, that all people have trouble getting out their words at some times. If the problem intensifies or persists, seek out professional help.

Notes...

INDIVIDUAL EDUCATION PLAN The "I E P"

I n Individualized Education Plan (IEP) is very helpful for directing efforts to make the most of available time and may be required by law in some states and situations. As mentioned before, an IEP is:

1. The child's current functioning level

2. A record of how that level was determined

3. Long term goals in any area targeted for improvement

4. Short term objectives stated in terms of steps to reach the goals

5. Methods and materials which will be used to implement the objectives

6. A statement of who is the person responsible to implement the stated goals. For a homeschooling parent, it is a guide of where you are coming from and where you are going, a record of when you get there, and the proof that you have been moving.

Let's look at each of the areas of the IEP.

Long term goals. This is where you really identify what is important to you and state your world view in terms of your child. Personally, I believe our standard is set out in Luke 2:52. "And Jesus increased in wisdom, in stature, and in favor with God and man." In other words, His childhood was filled with learning wisdom (not just information), growing physically, socially, and spiritually. Even simply listing the goal areas puts academic learning into a biblical perspective. A broad statement of long term goals for any child of any age might be: "My long term goal is that (child's name) would increase in wisdom, in stature, and in favor with God and man." This would be followed by an outline similar to the one on the next page.

This type of organization will help you keep in mind that academics are only a small part of the skills we want our children to learn. Then, when you only spend an hour or two in a given day on academics you will not have the guilt feelings that you have not "done your job." There are other things of equal or greater importance in life.

Wisdom

- Bible knowledge
- biblical principles
- academics
  - reading
  - language and spelling
  - literature
  - math
  - science
  - history
  - geography
  - the arts
  - music
  - visual arts
  - speech and dramatic skills

Stature

- health
- hygiene
- physical skills
  - individual
  - group sports

Favor with God

- personal relationship
- daily quiet time
- witnessing skills
- service

Favor with man

- home skills
- leisure skills
- job

173

Set two to four specific **objectives** under each of those headings. This will give you direction, identify the steps you are currently working on, and keep you focused. You can see at a glance what you hope to accomplish and have something to show others. See example on the following page.

Wisdom
- Bible Knowledge
  — John will be able to name the two parts of the Bible.
  — John knows the Old Testament has 39 books.
  — John can name the Old Testament books.
- Academics: Math
  — John will do 100 addition facts (80% correct) in 5 minutes.
  — John will add two 2-digit numbers with no renaming.
  — John will coutt and write numerals to 1,000.

Stature
- Hygiene
  — John will brush teeth, style hair, and dress without reminder.
  — John will use deodorant daily.
- Physical Skills: Balls
  — John will be able to toss and catch a beach ball.
  — John will throw and catch a softball.
  — John will throw and catch a football.

Favor With God
- Quiet Time
  — John will spend fifteen minutes daily reading the Bible.
  — John record prayer requests and dates of answers.
- Christlikeness
  — John will study and practice dependability.
  — John will study and practice gentleness.

Favor With Man

- Home Skills: Food
  - John will classify foods according to the food pyramid.
  - John will know which foods need refrigeration.
  - John will measure and pour liquids.
  - Clothing Care
  - John will sort clothes for laundry.
  - John will transfer clothes to dryer and start load.
  - John will fold and put away his own clothes.

When you have determined the specific objectives for each goal, decide what materials you will use for each. At times it may be easier to work from the materials to the objective. List the materials for each subject in the following manner: (These use made-up material's names.)

Math

John will do 100 addition facts (80%) in 5 minutes.

John will add two 2-digit numbers with no renaming.

John will count and write numerals to 1,000.

Pages 35-75 Mathematics Computation Course.

Computer Bunny Program Level 3.

Quiet Time

John will spend fifteen minutes daily reading the Bible.

Bible, Jr. Devotion Book

John will record prayer requests and dates of answers.

John's Prayer Journal

As John meets each goal, date the item and give the level of mastery (percentage of success). This may be done immediately on the completion of each goal, or at the end of the quarter or semester. At that time, set two to four new objectives in each area. If you are homeschooling in the unit study method, you may choose to relate all the objectives to the topic of study and evaluate at the end of the unit.

Obviously this will be easiest to keep on a computer. If you do not have access to that convenience, keep a separate page for each goal and add objectives as needed. Another possibility is to keep a notebook with a divider section for each goal. As you add to it, this becomes a record of his schoolwork that can be used to verify his progress. In the notebook, you can keep any tests which are administered and sample papers in the child's own handwriting. The author has developed a list of sequential objejectives for the above outline. This resource is called Lukes List and is anow vailable from Greenleaf Press.

Chapter
Twenty

Depression:
Causes and Cures

All of us face depression at times. As the parent or teacher of a hard to teach child, you are more than likely going to face times of depression. Our children who daily struggle to do what comes so easily to others are even more prone to suffer with depression. They will handle that time better if they are given some understanding of depression and some coping skills before they are caught in the negative thinking which is so much a part of depression.

This information is given so that you will have the tools to cope with depression and to give you what you need to teach your child about depression before he is bound in it.

Depression is a little like quicksand. It catches us unawares and drags us down. It can best be conquered with a good calm plan of escape made in advance.

Depression can be controlled. If it has been controlling you, it is curable.

Mental health is God's desire for everyone; it is therefore attainable. Take the time to put into practice good mental health habits, then teach them to your children.

Causes of Depression

1. **Exhaustion:** physical, mental, or emotional

   CURE: Rest; Physical (sleep, eat right, and exercise), mental (escapism; i.e. some mindless activity: reading a light book, fiddling with a hobby, getting out with a friend),emotional (cry, talk, read joyful psalms, pray with a friend). Read Elijah's story (I Kings 18:21-19:8). He successfully faced all the prophets of Baal, then ran from a woman's threat. He was exhausted! Solution? Sleep! Right Food! Corrected thinking!

2. **Stinking Thinking:** Dwelling on unhappy thoughts (past, guilt; things over which we have no control but try to control anyway).

CURE: Choose to control thinking. We, not God or satan, are the only ones who control what our mind dwells on. Phil. 4:8 says, "Whatsoever things are...good...think on these things." Choose to think about past successes, start a "Happiness is..." list and include things which you make happen, write a letter to cheer up a friend, do something to bless someone less fortunate than yourself, sing the Psalms, get involved in some activity you enjoy (sew or bake a gift, etc.) Get your mind on other things!

3. **Overwhelmed by Circumstances:** No one thing would get you down, but the combination of difficulties you are facing seems to be too much.

   CURE: Make a priority list of things you do have control over and begin to conquer one thing at a time. Whenever possible, start with something that will have visible, measurable results (typing a paper, washing the dishes, cheering someone). Mark each off the list as you complete it for sense of control and accomplishment. Note Genesis. God looked back at what He had done and said, "It is good." Now it's your turn. You do something, look back at it, and say. "It is good." If possible, leave the visible results of what you have done where you can see it for a few hours or days. Let these accumulate. Realize they wouldn't have been done if it hadn't been for you!

Delegate or decline. If you really have taken on more than you can handle, find someone else to help or just graciously get out of something you have committed to. This is a last resort, but occasionally NECESSARY! Do it without guilt for it is a common problem.

Remember God can use this thing in your life if you give it to Him. He is bigger than any mountain! What may seem awful right now may give you a whole new ministry in the future. Stop trying to eliminate pain from your life. All lives have it and it does **not** have to be THE ENEMY! On the other hand, neither do we have to create misery in our lives for God to use. Enough of it will happen on its own!

179

4. Loneliness: (Usually the result of stinking thinking.)

CURE: **Realize there are many others** who need your company as much as you need theirs. Find someone who does and begin to consider their needs! (Your spouse, a friend or relative, a child, a nursing home patient.) Spend time doing something with or for them. (Visit and find something cheerful to share with them, write a cheerful letter, make and send or deliver a gift.) I get great joy now and then by delivering flowers to five or ten people I think it would cheer up. I'm not wealthy, so I get them at bargain prices after a holiday or whenever I find a great bargain.

5. All time stolen by needs and none left for recreation: (Result of wrong priorities.)

CURE: **Immediate**: **(Take a** ten minute **mini-vacation** of the mind and sing a song, think cheerful thoughts, etc.) **Long-term**: Reorganize lifestyle to **include fun.** (Take a class you'd enjoy, begin a non-threatening, non-demanding hobby, schedule a favorite activity for the near future, or schedule something weekly that you enjoy.) Notice that at creation, God took time to cheer himself up. He looked at what He had done and said, "It is good." He rested every night between jobs and took one day out of seven to do something other than the routine. (Maybe we can learn from His example?!)

6. No reason to live: Nothing to look forward to. (Result of combination of the above)

CURE: First straighten out your thinking! See Depression Cause Number Two, then make sure you have one or two events scheduled in the future which you look forward to with a smile. (Don't grasp the individual event; then if it is cancelled or postponed, you will survive! Plan another immediately.) If one person continually lets you down, stop counting on them! Get some reliable people in your life. Be a reliable person for someone. Plan a party, plan a trip, plan an event or a night out, plan a happy surprise for someone who needs it. Plan some events to include others and some events alone. Part of the fun is the planning and anticipation.

7. Cyclical Depression: Triggered by a happening in our past on this date, hormonal changes, etc.

CURE: If hormonal, do what you can (see Number 8) and learn to live with it.

If triggered by past, write new memories over the old. **Plan a quiet pleasant activity at a time you know will be difficult.** When I was single, holidays were often lonely. Each year I chose a person or family to surprise. I planned for weeks. I invited them over for dinner before or after the holiday when they wouldn't be stressed. When they arrived, there were gifts and party treats, candles and music. (I always included a gift for me so they didn't feel awkward.) Their joy at being thought of in a special way made my holiday.

Enlist the help of someone you can trust. Tell them the times you know will be difficult and **plan events to include them.** Don't overwhelm yourself. Going out for dinner, or a picnic by the lake may be eventful enough. This must be a gradual change, but it will come eventually.

8. Physical Causes: (Low Blood Sugar, Hormones, etc.)

CURE: Don't forget, there are physical reasons for depression. If there is doubt, **consult a physician and follow his advice!**

When I lived in a small household of three, each one of us took a different medicine which, directly or indirectly, helped control moods. These were necessary to control medical deficiencies in our bodies and were essential to our good attitudes and ability to function in life.

9. Chronic Illness: It may not be the illness itself which causes the depression, but thinking about the early end of life, exhaustion, inability to do "normal" things with your family, etc.

CURE: First realize that nobody owes us a perfect life. No life is perfect. Then look for ways that this situation can be looked on as a blessing; meeting people who you wouldn't otherwise meet, ability to empathize with others

181

who have similar problems, more opportunity to pray, etc. Read biographies of Godly people who overcame great difficulty. Take courage from their strength.

10. **Overload:** There may not be any one thing which alone would overwhelm, but a combination of little and big things with which we can't seem to cope.

     CURE: Prioritize and Eliminate. Choose something which will respond to minimal effort, do that, and get it out of your life! (See Number Three.)

11. **Let Down:** After any major expenditure of adrenalin, expect a let down to occur. This may be anything from a fight with a spouse to company for dinner, a death in the family, a wedding of a daughter, or too much exercise.

     CURE: This is related to exhaustion. (See Depression Cause Number One.) Learn to anticipate and prepare for these normal let downs. Allow yourself a little **extra rest and a return to normal routine.** Realize that this **is** normal and temporary. Ride it out.

12. **Spiritual Causes:** There are times when the cause of our depression is in the spiritual realm. When it is, only spiritual answers will have lasting results.

     A. **Unconfessed Sin.** Is there unconfessed sin in your life?

        CURE: God says, "If you confess your sin, He is faithful and just to forgive us of our sins and to cleanse us from all unrighteousness." God cannot be otherwise. **If we confess, He forgives.** If you don't feel forgiven, change your stinking thinking! Don't expect God to be as faithless as others in your life have been - or as you yourself are. Remember, God is God. He is faithful! He <u>cannot</u> be different!

     B. **Unforgiving Heart.** Are you refusing to forgive?

        CURE: There is a strange reality about forgiveness. God was very aware of this reality when He told us to forgive. Jesus alluded to it when he said in the Lord's Prayer,

"Forgive us... as we forgive..." "As we forgive..." That says if we forgive, we shall be forgiven. Are you struggling to break sin's hold in your life? **If** we don't forgive, we shall go unforgiven! Sounds unfair, but it is another natural consequence. When we forgive, **we are changed**! Unforgiveness doesn't hurt the one you refuse to forgive; **unforgiveness hurts the one who refuses to forgive!** So make a conscious decision to **forgive!** Do it now! No matter what the hurt, no matter what the pain, God is bigger than that!! He will free you **when you forgive!**

C. **Not Responding to God's Call On Your Life.** Has God put a call on your life which you are refusing to answer? When God has asked us to do something (Take a cake to a neighbor, forgive someone, go to Bangladesh as a missionary), He won't remove that call from our life.

   CURE: It may be that the opportunity to obey has passed. In that case, we must confess the sin of rebellion. If the opportunity remains, **begin to obey!** God can redirect if He so chooses now that He has our attention and our willingness to be led.

D. **No Quiet Time.** Are you neglecting a private time with the Lord, reading His Word and praying for His guidance and wisdom?

   CURE: How can you expect to feel happy when you spend no time with the Source of Happiness? That is like expecting an electric iron to heat up when it is not plugged in! Find a good devotional guide and begin immediately to consistently use it!

E. **Spiritual Warfare.** Are you engaged in spiritual warfare? The enemy is attacking. He has many avenues.

   CURE: We have only one defense: the Word of God! We must know God and the precedences He has set up in His Word so well that we can discern when to resist the devil so he will flee, when to quote scripture to him as

Jesus did during his temptation, when to avoid all appearance of evil, and when to flee. **Get back to your quiet time** and look to God for wisdom! James 1:5 "If any man lacks wisdom, he has only to ask of God, **and it shall be given!**" God cannot be faithless! He said it. He'll do it!

F. **Sin's Bondage.** Are you struggling to break sin's hold in your life? A pattern of sin has a tremendous grip. Even after you have confessed and forsaken the sin itself, there will be reminders in your life and in your thinking. Lifestyle reminders are the natural consequences of our sin; the child you conceived out of wedlock and are now raising, the criminal record which now follows you everywhere you go, the empty bank account which you gambled away.

CURE: Whenever possible, remove these reminders from your life; gradually replace the savings, etc. When this is not possible, transform your thinking about them: Use these people, events, things or thoughts as reminders that **God has forgiven you and you now live a new life.** "Behold, old things are passed away, all things are become new." Each time these reminders come into your sight or mind, thank God that you "don't live that way anymore." Rejoice with Him that you have forsaken that lifestyle. Look for people who have been hurt in the same way to whom you can minister

Godly guilt is given by the Father to lead you to confession. With this kind of guilt you have actually done something which you need to bring to God for confession.

Godly guilt has a cure. It is called confession. Do it! False guilt is given by the enemy to make you impotent in the Kingdom of God. Recognize it for what it is and shake free from its grasp! The Bible says there is now no condemnation. Condemnation leads to guilt. Guilt leads to oppression. Oppression leads to bondage. Bondage suffocates. God does not condemn. If you are sensing condemnation, it is **not** from God. God in the person of the Holy Spirit convicts us of sin in our lives. Conviction leads naturally to repentance and confession. Godly repentance leads to forgiveness. Forgiveness leads to joy.

Are you under condemnation? It is not from God. Resist the devil and he will flee from you. Are you under conviction? Repent, confess, and allow the Spirit of God to bathe you in His forgiveness and joy. If you are feeling guilt and are not sure which it is, ask yourself:

- Are you guilty? Did you do something you need to confess? If so, do so.

- Does someone else have a wounded spirit you may have caused? If so, humbly ask forgiveness.

- Are you totally unable to pray about this? Does God seem far away? Talk to Him. Ask Him to reveal the matter. Name the offense and ask Him to cleanse the situation.

- If you have done the above and are still feeling guilt, it is satan's tactic. Bow before God, lift your head high to satan and go on about the life of peace God has given you.

God holds forgiveness within your grasp.

Reach out and receive Him. What if you have been working on getting depression out of your life and are not seeing results?

First, look at the above, especially possible physical causes. Deal with them as much as possible. Second, grab onto small signs of **success**! Magnify them. Use them as a reason to **celebrate**! When the times of depression are further apart, or less intense, or don't last as long, take this as a sign that you are becoming healthy and begin to see yourself as a mentally healthy individual. **Learn to celebrate small successes!** Don't wait until you are "never depressed" to think of yourself as happy.

Other Good Practices For Mental Health

Do What You Can

Maybe you can't change another's unhappy life, but you can **give** them **a few moments of peace.** Maybe you can't move to a better neighborhood, but you can **plant some flowers** in a box. Look for ways to **quietly and simply improve your situation.** Then do it!

Have a Friend

Scout around. **Find a person** who has a lifestyle that is healthy and has time to add something fun. Cultivate them.

Be a Friend

Do something friendly. Go out of your way to do something nice for someone. Take a plate of cookies, mend a tear, write a note, send a little gift. Notice the good feelings you get and enjoy those feelings.

Keep Something Before You

Always have something to look ahead to. Plan some fun in the future.

Positive Thinking

So much has been said by so many about positive thinking that I hesitate to add more. Positive thinking should not mean mind control or controlling God by our demands. It is, however, important to try to **see the good in people and events in our lives.**

Humor

Read the jokes in *Reader's Digest* and *Saturday Evening Post* and *Good Housekeeping.* Laughing **at** someone is feeling superior and making them the object of ridicule. Laughing **with** them is recognizing how like you they are!

Lack of Clutter

Clutter tends to cause depression. **Clean up** as much as possible. Get rid of what you don't need. Give to the needy or have a garage sale. Sort, organize, and simplify whenever possible.

Read of Other's – Triumphs Over Adversity

We can often renew our spirits by seeing what others have overcome. *Guideposts* is an excellent source of uplifting true stories of people who overcome. **Biographies** are available from the library or your local Christian bookstore.

Clear Conscience

As much as possible, **don't do what you will have to apologize for later.** Do apologize when you recognize you've made a mistake, hurt someone, or failed to keep a promise. Don't live a life full of apology. Don't make promises that you may not be able to keep. Explain in advance that you plan to do something, but you may not be able to control the circumstances. Admit the possibility that you may not be able to keep a promise.

Find Something to Nurture

Nurture a person whenever possible. This has the greatest rewards. Children, nursing home residents, neighbors, and single adults are good investments of our time and love. If that is not possible as a lifestyle, nurture a plant or a pet. In general, it is not healthy to honor plants, animals, and inanimate objects above people. If you cannot nurture in person, bathe someone in your prayers and send them a lot of cheerful mail.

Surround Yourself With Beauty

Your **environment** (home, auto, workplace) should be as much as possible **clean, uncluttered and attractive.** If that is beyond your control, have a little thing of beauty you can rest your eyes on frequently.

Take Regular Mini-vacations

A mini-vacation can be **a moment** of happy thought in the middle of the work day, a whistled tune while you spruce up the room, **an hour** at the beach or in the woods, **a day** of relaxation, or **a weekend** away from it all.

Write Cheery Thank You Notes

We all appreciate appreciation. Find things to be thankful for, discern who helped it happen. **Let them know you noticed.**

Search your past for the people who have done things that were helpful to you. Write a note and let someone know you remember.

Stop Trying to Control

We have no power over other people and many of the events in our lives. Don't try to control all the happenings in your life or your family; **control your response to them instead.** Become a controlled, healthy person instead of a controlling, neurotic one.

Develop a Mentally Healthy Lifestyle

Get enough rest. Eat right. Get moderate exercise. Learn to be thankful for what **is**, instead of wishing for what isn't. Depression is a temporary state natural for every human being. It does not have to be an enemy, but it is not a desirable lifestyle. Depression is only life-threatening when you allow it to take control.

REMEMBER:

Depression is the body's way of saying that something is wrong, like a red warning light. Figure out what it is and deal with it!

Resource Guide

Throughout this Resource Guide, I will suggest books which I have found to meet needs for parents who are interested in furthering their children's education. These are suggestions only. No book is perfect (even this one!) and each has its own slant. Where possible, I give the ISBN number. When that is not possible, I give the company address for you to contact directly. Many of these materials can also be ordered from Lifetime Books and Gifts. Where that is true, their catalog order number (in the form #ABC-1234) is given. This is not to say that you must order from them, but having one source for several items may save you time. For more information about these items and for a complete catalog, write Lifetime Books and Gifts, 3900 Chalet Suzanne Drive, Lake Wales, FL 33853-7763. If you prefer, you may call (for information 813-676-6311) (for orders only 1-800-377-0390).

To Train Him In The Way

📖 **To Train Up A Child,** Michael and Debi Pearl
No ISBN
This is a treasure of an education in the differences between training and discipline. We need to incorporate more of these ideas with all of our children. Don't be put off by one or two ideas you don't like — adopt the ones you can. Tomorrow's society will be better off for it!

📖 **For Instruction in Righteousness,** Forster
No ISBN #DOR-0006
Scriptures and application to correct many behaviors.

189

📖   **Under**   **Loving**   **Command,**   Fabrizio
No ISBN #   S   H   E   -   0   7   0   5   P
Tiny treasure on biblical discipline.

Legal Information

❖ **HSLDA** (Home School Legal Defense Association)
P.O. Box 159 Paeonian Springs, VA 22129
Provides information packet for families who are educating
special needs children including curriculum sources and other
resources. Refers to consultants if needed. Puts out a bi-month-
ly newsletter and provides legal defense for members.

❖ **NICHCY** (National Information Center for Children and
Youth with Disabilities), PO Box 1492, Washington, D.C.
20013-1492,
1-800-695-0285.
Marvelous free fact sheets and informative up-to-date bul-
letins on specific topics as well as resources state by state.
See order form at the end of this section.

Support Groups

❖ **NATHHAN**
NATional cHallenged Homeschoolers Association Network
5383 Alpine Road S.E., Olalla, WA 98359, 206-857-4257.
A network for families homeschooling special needs children
which connects you with another family, provides resources
and an inspiring and informative newsletter.

❖ **C.H.A.D.D.**
Children and Adults with Attention Deficit Disorders
499 N.W. 70th Avenue, Suite 102, Plantation, FL 33317
305-792-8944
Secular support organization with local groups all over
the country for families dealing with ADD and ADHD.
Produces semi-annual magazine, monthly newsletter, and
other resources.

Magazines

- **The Teaching Home** — Box 20219, Portland, OR 97220
  Issues June, July 1990 and July, August 1994 feature special education. Magazine has articles to help newcomers or old-timers in homeschooling.

- **Homeschooling Today** — P. O. Box 1425, Melrose, FL 32666
  Features read-it-today, use-it-tomorrow articles.

- **Homemade Schooling** — R.R.1, Box 188, Atwood, IL 61913
  Informative newsletter for families homeschooling a special needs child, includes inspiration and usable ideas.

- **Practical HomeSchooling** — P.O. Box 1250, Fenton, MO 63026
  Regular features on phonics, teen education, unit studies, history and more, with lots of product reviews by Mary Pride.

General Education

- **Special Education:** *A Biblical Approach*, Sutton, Ed.
  ISBN 0963-4315-01   #HTC-0001P
  Beautifully gives the heart of educating special needs children with a biblical outlook. Directed toward those in Christian schools, but has many helps for anyone.

- **The Parent's Guide to Attention Deficit Disorder,** Hawthrone
  1-800-542-1673
  Hawthorne Educational Services, Inc., 800 Gray Oak Drive, Columbia, MO 65201
  Identifies 188 learning problems and gives 20 to 50 strategies for each which are designed to build success.

- **Classroom Success for the Learning Disabled,** Stevens
  ISBN 089587-035-5   #III-6929P
  Wonderful information on adjusting academic demands to meet the needs of the different learner. Especially appropriate for the older student.

📖 **Understanding Learning Disabilities:** *How Difficult Can This Be?* Video by PBS
Makes you feel the frustration, anger and tension of the learning disabled! Gives you a look at visual and auditory perception, memory, and language processing.

📖 **7 Laws of the Learner, How to Teach Almost Anything to Practically Anyone!** Wilkinson
ISBN 0-88070-464-9 #III-6601H
Wonderful resource on learning and teaching from a biblical perspective. This book will inspire and challenge you!

📖 **Helping Children Overcome Learning Difficulties,**
Rosner
ISBN 0-8027-7396-6 #III-6934P
Helps you understand and build specific skills in math, language, visual and auditory perception.

📖 **How to Really Love Your Child,** Campbell
ISBN 045-116-8356 #III-0685P
Provides many innovative ways to express love to a child.

📖 **I Always, Always have Choices!,** Kondracki
ISBN 080-075-4409 #III-6720P
Helps the whole family look at options instead of feeling there is no way out.

📖 **How To Rescue At Risk Students,** Stevens
ISBN 1-878419-00-5 #III-6930P
Turn a student from failure to success with these very practical helps.

📖 **Helping the LD Student with Homework,** Stevens
ISBN 1-878419-01-3 #III-6932P
This will teach you how to get your child to work independently!

📖 **Enabling Disorganized Students to Succeed,** Stevens
ISBN 1-878419-02-1 #III-6931P
Essential for increasing productivity of disorganized learners. My husband loved this one!

192

For the Student to Read

📖 **Survival Guide for Kids with LD,** Fisher
ISBN 0-915793-18-0   #III-6933P
How to handle problems at home, in school and socially.
Written for the 8-12 year old to read or have read to him.

📖 **Survival Guide for Teenagers with LD,** Fisher
ISBN 0-915793-51-2   #III-6953P
Covers job, career, and social skills for the teen plus more!

Pertinent Biographies

📖 **Uncommon Gift,** Evans
ISBN 0-664-27009-3   #III-0652H
Autobiography of a dyslexic. Must reading for the family of
anyone struggling to learn. Read it aloud!

📖 **Michael Faraday,** Ludwig
ISBN 8361-1864-2   #III-6954P
The *Father of Electronics* overcame a speech impediment to
go on to be a famous scientist and speaker. Even the royal
English family regularly attended his science lectures!

📖 **Catching Their Talk In A Box,** Hockett
ISBN 0-943-701-13-9 #IHTC-0001P
An absent-minded student becomes a missionary who
starts a recording studio.

📖 **Ben Carson,** Carson
ISBN 0-310-58641-0   #III-6718P
As a child, Ben was bottom in his class. Today he's a famous
pediactric neuro-surgeon.

📖 **Guideposts Magazine**
P.O. Box 856, Carmel, NY 10512-0856
This fine magazine routinely includes stories of people who
conquer insurmountable odds to succeed in life.

Mastery List of Skills

📖 **Luke's List,** Herzog
ISBN 0-89-826-0442   #FCP-0001P
Greenleaf Press
3761 Highway 109N, Unit D, Lebanon, TN 37087
This is a list of specific skills according to the outline of Luke 2:52 on page 163, and includes objectives for spiritual, academic, physical, home, leisure, and job growth.. *Luke's List* is available and will be published by Greenleaf Press.

I E P

📖 **How to Write An IEP,** Arena
ISBN 087-879-8722   #III-7018P
Helps you develop an IEP

📖 **Allergies**
Is This Your Child? *Discovering and Treating Unrecognized Allergies In Children and Adults,* Rapp
ISBN 0688-11907-7   #III-7090P
Some learning problems are allergy related. Rule this out before going on to more severe treatments!

Learning Styles

📖 **Learning Styles and Tools**
ISBN 0-89826-046-9   #FCP-0002P
The best book I've seen on identifying your teaching style and the student's learning styles and what to do about it. See Cathy Duffy's Christian Home Educators' Curriculum Manuals on page 187.

📖 **Shifters:** *How to Help Children Concentrate,* Stevens
ISBN 1-878419-03-X   #III-6952P
Suggestions for including left and right brain activities in your lessons.

194

📖 **Treasure Tree:***Helping Kids Get Along and Enjoy Each Other,* Smalley
ISBN   084-990-9368
Word Publishing Co. Book for children on learning styles using animal's personalities to aid understanding.

📖 **More Parents are Teachers, Too,** Jones
ISBN   0-913589-43-8
Some information on learning styles, lots of activities to do with your child.

📖 **Seven Ways of Teaching,** David Lazear
ISBN   0-932935-32-X
Skylight Publishing, Palatine, IL 60067
Teaching with multiple intelligences.

Speech and Language Development

📖 **Straight Talk**, by Marisa Lapish
No ISBN #STS-0001
5301 W. Loveland Road, Madison, OH 44057
Excellent book and video enable you to correct your child's mispronounciations at home. If you have questions about your child's speech, this is for you!

📖 **Language and Thinking for Young Children**, Beechick
ISBN 0-88062-152-4   #MOT-1358P
A program for 4-6 year olds (special needs up to eight or nine) that is simple to use and fun for the children.

📖 **The Language of Toys**
ISBN 0933-1490-85   #III-6924 P
Wonderful suggestions for using many kinds of toys in early language development.

Vision Therapy

📖 **How To Teach Your Child To Read And Spell Successfully,**
Sheldon R. Rappaport, PhD
No ISBN #EES-0001P
Effective Educational Systems, Inc., 164 Ridgecrest Road, Heber Springs, AR 72543
This book is the best I've seen for giving the first step in identifying and eliminating visual or auditory perception problems. With it you will know whether you need additional help or can benefit from the exercises given.

📖 **Learning Connection,** Shapiro
ISBN 0962-4688-00   #III-7022P
Gives activities for developing visual skills at home.

📖 **College of Optometrists in Vision Development,**
National Office
PO Box 285, Chula Vista, CA 91912-0285
619-425-6191 • FAX 619-425-0733
Referral to specialists trained in vision development.

📖 **Parents Active for Vision Education, PAVE**
9620 Chesapeake Drive, San Diego, CA, 92123
610-467-9620 • FAX 619- 467-9624
Free Information and Video ($35 plus S&H).

Big Picture

❖ **SIMPLIFIED Learning Products,** featuring other books by Joyce Herzog
1-800-745-8212
  Scaredy Cat Reading System
  History in His Hands, Volume I
  History in His Hands, Volume II
  Stepping Stones to Bigger Faith for Little People
  Choosing and Using Curriculum For Your Special Child
  Luke's List
  Single Serving Recipes

ADD

📖 **The Parent's Guide to Attention Deficit Disorder**
Hawthorne Educational Services, Inc., 800 Gray Oak Drive, Columbia, MO 65201. This great resource has hundreds of strategies to reverse or reduce 46 behaviors related to ADD.

📖 **Maybe You Know My Kid! A Parents' Guide To Identifying, Understanding and Helping Your Child With Attention-Deficit Hyperactivity Disorder,** Fowler
ISBN   1-55972-209-6
Birch Lane Press, (Carol Publishing Group)
This is a treasure of understanding and help. If you know anyone with an overactive infant, toddler, or preschooler, give them this book before they develop all the negative behaviors it chronicles! This book describes one families struggle, but is filled with expert opinions, specific interventions, plus definite suggestions for what doesn't help or even increases the difficulty. Each chapter is summarized and includes such things as effective and ineffective parenting techniques, social interactions, management techniques, improving access, adolescence and adulthood, providing environmental access, and appreciation of individuals with AD/HD.

📖 *Maybe You Know My Kid!/A Parents' Guide to Identifying, Understanding and Helping Your Child with Attention-Deficit Hyperactivity Disorder,* by
Mary Fowler
ISBN 1-55972-209-6
236 pages plus index, paperback, $12.95
Birch Lane Press, (Carol Publishing Group)
This is a treasure of understanding and help. If you know anyone with an overactive infant, toddler, or preschooler, give them this book **before** they develop all the negative behaviors it chronicles! This book describes one family's struggle, but is filled with expert opinions, specific interventions, plus definite suggestions for what doesn't help or even increases the difficulty. Each chapter is summarized and includes such

things as effective **and** ineffective parenting techniques, social interactions, management techniques, improving access, adolescence and adulthood, providing environmental access, and appreciation of individuals with ADHD.

📖 **The Hyper Active Child,** Dr. Grant Martin
ISBN 0-89693-068-8
This is the most helpful general book I have found and it is from a Christian perspective! Many helpful definitions, hints,and resources. SImply put, it emphasizes unconditional love combined with training through games and carefully controlled discipline.

📖 *The Parent's Guide to Attention Deficit Disorder,*
McCarmey and Bauer (No ISBN)
Hawthorne Educational Services, Inc.
800 Gray Oak Drive
Columbia, MO 65201
This great resource lists 188 behaviors related to ADD and/or other problems of childhood. It then gives 20 to 50 strategies to reverse or reduce each behaviors. It is an essential book! According to the current popular thinking, it concentrates on positive rewards and eliminates discipline or punishment. You need both. It is, however, a wealth of material on setting up the environment and rewarding. Neither of these books is from a particularly Christian perspective, but I have not found anything offensive and they are thoroughly practical and extremely helpful.
If you have a young child and want to prevent these destructive behaviors from developing, another book may be extremely helpful. It is:*To Train Up a Child,* Mike and Debi Pearl.
This book teaches the difference between training and discipline and how to implement training before discipline is needed. This strategy is what is used in many Mennonite and Amish homes and explains why so many of them have six to ten stairstep children all almost perfectly behaved to our amazement and wonder. It is written in a humorous

way, yet holds many very helpful hints.
All of these books can be obtained directly from the publisher
or from Lifetime Books and Gifts Always Incomplete Resource
Guide and Catalog (1-800-377-0390) for orders or write:
Lifetime Books and Gifts
3900 Chalet Suzanne Drive
Lake Wales, FL 33853-7763
(ask for catalog number eight)
If you yourself struggle with directing your attention and
organizing your own life, there is a book which may help.

  📖 ***Adult ADD Workbook,*** by Lynn Weiss, Ph. D.
ISBN 0-87833-850-0
(85 pages, $17.95)
Taylor Publishing Company
1550 West Mockingbird Lane
Dallas, TX 75235
This is **not** a Christian book and has a few paragraphs
which I personally find very offensive (re: handling sexual
tensions and other morality), but the remainder of the book
is well done and would be quite beneficial to older teens and
adults who continue to struggle to conquer inattention. The
accompanying text book is like many others and would only
be helpful if you are new to the topic.

  📖 An article in a recent issue of **NATHHAN** (NATional
cHallenged Homeschoolers Associated Network) News is of
particular interest to Christian parents. Titled *The
Christian Home and ADHD,* it was written by a
Christian pediatrician and his wife who is a special educa-
tion teacher. It gives a Biblical approach to raising children
who have a hard time concentrating. It would benefit any
Christian family! **Please request and read this article.**
The Magazine can be obtained by writing:
NATHHAN
5383 Alpine Rd. SE
Olalla, WA 98359
Ask for the Fall 1995 Issue. Cost of back issues is $3.75. If

you are homeschooling a child like this, or any child with "special needs," you would benefit from belonging to this organization.

In summary, it is most important that you love and enjoy your child, whatever else you may do. Try to have at least one happy successful experience with him every day. Remember that he is a child and you are the adult. Play board games to increase his attention span, his social skills, and his decision making ability. Read to him. Play with him. Roughhouse with him. Cook together. Go swimming. Take a walk. Ride bikes. Teach him. Train him. Lead him in the way he should go. Find ways to enjoy him and the person he is becoming. Treasure these days while he is a child. He won't be for long!

Home Education

Why To Home School:

  📖 **Why So Many Christians Are Going Home To School,** Davis
ISBN 1-884098-00-2   #ELI-0656P
The reasons for choosing to homeschool and the explanations for doubtful relatives.

  📖 **The Right Choice: Homeschooling,** Chris Klicka
ISBN 0-923463-83-6   #CLW-1019P
The facts about the failure of public school from an academic, historical, practical, and legal perspective. Wonderful for convincing doubtful relatives!

How To Home School:

  📖 **How to Homeschool:** *A Practical Approach,* Graham
ISBN 1-880892-40-5   #FAM-2149P
The heart and how-to of homeschooling.

200

Curriculum

📖 **Christian Home Educators' Curriculum Manual, Elementary Grades,** Duffy
ISBN 0-929320-03-4 #HOM-0587P
How to choose curriculum including information on learning styles; planning, organizing, and scheduling your homeschool; curriculum recommendations in every subject. A wonderful resource!

📖 **Christian Home Educators' Curriculum Manual, High School,** Duffy
ISBN 0-929320-04-2 #HOM-0588P
How to choose curriculum including information on learning styles; planning, organizing, and scheduling your homeschool; curriculum recommendations in every subject. A wonderful resource for high school!

📑 **The Always Incomplete Resource Guide and Catalog**
Lifetime Books and Gifts, 3900 Chalet Suzanne Drive, Lake Wales, FL 33853-7763
This is your resource for inspirational and informative books as well as curriculum materials for special education and homeschooling. Joyce Herzog, author of *Learning In Spite of Labels,* has reviewed hundreds of books in various aspects of special needs, the best of which are which are available through this resource. Ask for Catalog Number 8. If there is a number in the following form (#ABC-1234), it is the identification number for ordering from Lifetime Books and Gifts.

📑 **The Greenleaf Press Catalog**
1-800-311-1508
3761 Highway 109, Unit D, Lebanon, TN 37087
Specializing in History, Art, Music,and Nature Study and the publishers of this book (and other books by Joyce Herzog). This catalog is free. Get yours today by calling the toll free number above and requesting one.

Notes...

NICHCY

National Information Center for Children and Youth with Disabilities
P.O. Box 1492, Washington, D.C. 20013-1492
1-800-695-0285 (Toll-Free, Voice/TT)
*SpecialNet User Name: NICHCY ** SCAN User Name: NICHCY*

PUBLICATIONS LIST 1993

NICHCY provides free information to assist parents, educators, caregivers, advocates, and others in helping children and youth with disabilities become participating members of the school and community. *NICHCY* also has material in Spanish. *NICHCY* can also provide personal responses to specific questions. To find out more about our full range of information and referral services, contact *NICHCY* and ask to speak to one of our Information Specialists. We will be pleased to send you additional information and resources.

Single copies of NICHCY materials are FREE. Permission to duplicate NICHCY materials is not required. In fact, we encourage duplication; however, please credit NICHCY as the source of the material.

Send information in: ___ **English** ___ **Spanish**

GENERAL RESOURCE

___ GR1 Brochure *
___ GR2 National Resources
___ GR3 General Information about Disabilities *
___ GR4 Public Agencies Fact Sheet
___ GR5 National Toll Free Numbers
___ GR6 State Resource Sheet: State
___ GR8 Publications List

NEWS DIGEST

___ ND11 Children with Disabilities: Understanding Sibling Issues
___ ND12 Respite Care: A Gift of Time
___ ND13 Assistive Technology: Becoming an Informed Consumer
___ ND14 Having a Daughter with a Disability: Is it Different for Girls?
___ ND15 The Education of Children and Youth With Special Needs: What Do the Laws Say? (Vol. I. No.1, 1991)
___ ND16 Related Services for School-aged Children with Disabilities (Vol. I. No. 2, 1991)
___ ND17 Sexuality Education for Children and Youth with Disabilities (Vol. I. No. 3, 1992)
___ ND18 Estate Planning (Vol. II. No. 1, 1992)
___ ND19 Promising Practices & Future Trends for Special Education (Vol. II, No. 2, 1993)
___ ND20 Parenting a Child with Special Needs: A Guide to Readings and Resources (Vol. III, No. 1, 1993)
___ ND21 Questions & Answers about the Individuals with Disabilities Education Act (IDEA) (Vol. III. No. 2, 1993)
___ ND22 Directory of Organizations (Vol. III, No. 3, 1993)

TRANSITION SUMMARY

___ TS5 Self Determination
___ TS6 Vocational Assessment
___ TS7 Options After High School for Youth with Disabilities
___ TS8 Transition Services in the IEP

DISABILITY INFORMATION

___ FS1 Autism *
___ FS2 Cerebral Palsy *
___ FS3 Deafness *
___ FS4 Down Syndrome *
___ FS5 Emotional Disturbance *
___ FS6 Epilepsy *
___ FS7 Learning Disabilities *
___ FS8 Mental Retardation *
___ FS9 Physical Disabilities & Special Health Problems
___ FS10 Severe and/or Multiple Disabilities
___ FS11 Speech and Language Impairments
___ FS12 Spina Bifida *
___ FS13 Visual Impairments *
___ FS14 Attention Deficit Disorder (Briefing Paper)
___ FS17 Reading and Learning Disabilities Resource Guide
___ FS18 Traumatic Brain Injury *

MATERIALS FOR PARENTS

___ PA2 Parents' Guide to Accessing Programs for Infants, Toddlers, Preschoolers w/Disabilities (ages 0-5) *
___ PA6 A Parent's Guide: Accessing the ERIC Resource Collection
___ PA7 A Parent's Guide to Doctors, Disabilities, and the Family
___ PA8 A Parent's Guide: Planning a Move: Mapping Your Strategy
___ PA9 A Parent's Guide: Special Education and Related Services: Communicating Through Letter Writing (Vol II, No. 1, Sept. 1991)
___ PA10 A Parent's Guide: Accessing Parent Groups

OTHER

___ ADT Resources for Adults with Disabilities
___ LG1 Questions Often Asked About Special Education Services (ages 3-21) *

* Available in Spanish

(see other side)

203

Please complete the following:

What age ranges are you interested in?
(Please circle all ages that apply)

    0-2   3-5   6-12   13-18

      19-22   23-over   All ages

Have you contacted NICHCY before?

____ Yes   ____ No

____ I am already on the NICHCY mailing list
or
____ Place my name on the mailing list to receive:

    ____ **NEWS DIGEST** (only)
    ____ **TRANSITION SUMMARY** (only)
    ____ **NEWS DIGEST and TRANSITION SUMMARY**

Check the one that best describes you:

____ Parent/Family Member
____ Educational Professional
____ Other Professional
____ Advocate
____ Adult with Disabilities
____ Student with Disabilities
____ Able-bodied Student
____ Parent Organization/Group
____ Library/Information Center
____ Other (specify _____)

What disability are you interested in?

_____
_____
_____

PLEASE TYPE OR PRINT:

First Name   Last Name

Organization (for mailing list purposes only)

Address

City   State   Zip Code   Day Telephone (Area Code & Number)

If you have additional questions or would like to provide any additional information or comments, please feel free to enclose a letter or brief note!

The National Information Center for Children and Youth with Disabilities (NICHCY) is a national information and referral clearinghouse. NICHCY operates through the Clearinghouse Program, authorized by Section 633 of Part D of the Individuals with Disabilities Education Act, (20 U.S.C. 1433), as amended by Public Law 102-476.

NICHCY is operated by the Academy for Educational Development, pursuant to Cooperative Agreement #H030A30003 with the Office of Special Education Programs. The contents of this publication do not necessarily reflect the views or policies of the Department of Education, nor does mention of trade names, commercial products, or organizations imply endorsement by the U. S. Government.

UPDATE 12/93

Mail to: **NICHCY, P.O. Box 1492, Washington, D.C. 20013-1492**

Appendix B

Author Information

Joyce Herzog began tutoring when she was in the second grade! Already at this age she was given to the privilege of assisting struggling students in her own classroom and in lower grades. It was also at this time that she decided to become a professional teacher.

Joyce was in her element as a student. But, when she finally left the protective walls of school, it was a shock to her to discover that she had never developed the necessary social and personal skills to understand or function in "real life". The years of concentrated effort were necessary.

When she first began to teach, she also worked with an optometrist in the field of children's vision therapy. She had been on high-risk car insurance. They accidentally discovered that she had no depth perception. This responded readily to therapy, and she has had no car accidents since — over 20 years.

Joyce earned her BA degree from Hope College in Holland, Michigan, and began teaching "special students" before any laws regarding learning disabilities (LD) were written. Years later LD began to emerge as a separate speciality, so Joyce earned her M.A. in Learning Disabilities from the University of Iowa. Joyce has accumulated twenty-five years of professional experience in teaching. Nineteen years were in the public schools in Illinois and Iowa; seventeen of those were in LD resource rooms. Six years were in private Christian schools and several others as well. Joyce developed and implemented the LD program in every position she held, including two pre-schools, a summer camp, and one county with three separate districts.

Joyce married late in life and had only one pregnancy which miscarried. Still, her parental experiences with children are impressive. Single into her early thirties, she wanted to be a parent, and became one of the first single foster parents in her area. Her first foster child stayed until high school graduation and marriage. The second child placed with her was a pregnant girl of fifteen. She remained with Joyce through the pregnancy. After two months of being a mommy, she decided to place her baby in an adoptive home. Joyce also was mom to three emotionally abused siblings who had been in three other homes in the previous twelve months. She has often been called on to be a short term nanny for large families, very young or high risk infants, and other situations which called for expertise.

Joyce developed The Scaredy Cat Reading System during her years in the classroom. She and her husband have been publishing, producing, and marketing it throughout the United States since 1990. She has exhibited and presented workshops at homeschool conventions from Denver to Orlando to Columbus, Ohio. Since 1984, Joyce has provided consultations for homeschooling families with special needs children.

In 1993-94, Joyce reviewed hundreds of books in every area of special education for Lifetime Books and Gifts, a major provider of home education materials.

Joyce holds a Permanent Professional Certificate in the state of Iowa to teach elementary (K-9) with an endorsement in learning disabilities. She has been a member of the Council for Exceptional Children (CEC) for many years, and she is featured in Who's Who In American Education.

Leaving professional teaching in 1990, she and her husband were free to provide home-care for both of her parents during the final two years of their lives. Their combined illnesses included terminal Alzheimers , cancer, advanced diabetes with its complications, heart, lung and kidney disease. In spite of the difficulties of daily care, there were treasured times and both parents were led to the LORD as a direct result of this ministry.

Now step-parent to seven adults, she continues to devote her time and heart to working with other people and their children. Joyce and her husband, Tom, occasionally live with their dog Nikki, and two cats, in St. Augustine, Florida, the oldest city in the United States. At other times, they may be found living in their motor home in backyards and parking lots, and traveling between conferences and assignments.

AFTERWORD

Will this book ever be finished? Of course! I've finished it four times already and that only takes into account this week! No, I think, like the Always Incomplete Catalog and Resource Guide, this will never be finished. The Billys and Susans are still teaching me...and now they are teaching you as well. Perhaps ten or twenty years from now you will be writing your book! Take copious notes now even though there really is absolutely no time, because you'll appreciate it later, whether for your own nostalgia, or as the nuggets for your own book.

Two things I want to say before this "final" version goes to print.

I guess it is obvious that I lean toward homeschooling. It wasn't always so. Many years ago, I said that parents of learning disabled children should leave the teaching to the experts. "Keep the 'Mommy' relationship at home and leave the struggle with learning to me," I would say. I really believed that then. Now I realize that many children are being destroyed in the first few years of school. Some never recover. Academics are stressed, demands and comparisons are made, and self-esteem is so trounced that even the best teaching can't reverse the situation. A mom can understand her child, and God's call on his life better than any teacher can. A mom can sense when her child has really had enough and has the power to back off and let him have some space.

A teacher is limited by the demands of the curriculum, space, and number of students. Even an excellent teacher with years of experience, struggles with the demands of the classroom and is unable to adapt to the needs of every child. If GOD had wanted children educated in groups of thirty similar only in chronological age, babies would be born in litters! Huge litters at that! Did you ever notice that, left to GOD, babies come one at a time, and by the time there is a fifth or sixth, there is a built in "teacher's aide?"

This is not to belittle the job being done by many dedicated Christian teachers both in public and Christian schools. Praise GOD for them. There are many reasons why some children will not be educated in the home. And there is much missionary work being done in public and Christian schools. But after twenty-five years in the system, I know too well the limitations of the classroom. While I believe God's original design for education was the family, I pray that GOD will bless the teachers who truly care wherever they are found!

As I sit here working at 3:30 a.m., my husband has just quit working on the index and has gone to bed for a few hours of sleep before he gets up to face it again. I'm just getting up with another "creative mode", a common excuse for sleeplessness in our home. I learned something yesterday that I think is important to share. When I got up in the morning, there was a note from my husband Tom, on my desk. It told me that there had been another computer glitch in the page jumps and he had had to start the index over for the fourth time this week! I was devastated. We had worked so hard and were so close to the deadline. He had the index half finished (more than fifteen hours of our work) on Tuesday at 7 a.m. Then came the first glitch to affect the index. For the first time in our personal computer history, one of us (we'll never know who) made a fatal error that totally destroyed and lost forever the entire document. Twice after that I added or edited enough to change all his page numbers and he cheerfully started over. Now, a fourth time he had faced the same situation. He was sleeping. I found his note and broke down. I spent two hours in misery, unable to think, work, or sleep. Finally, he got up and said, "Oh, don't worry. I already worked three hours after that and am caught up to where I was. It's no big deal."

"No big deal?" I had worried, cried, planned to abort all future plans and maybe even give up the idea of finishing the book, but it was no "big deal?!"

Then he made another of his profound observations:

"You didn't need to worry about that. GOD didn't give you grace to do my job. He only gave you the grace to do yours."

Simple, but profound. I didn't have GOD's grace to do Tom's work. Then I thought of the many ways this simple statement affects you.

You have GOD's grace to do your job. You will have no grace to do your child's job, or your husband's job, or any other job that GOD has not called you to do. If GOD's call is on you to educate your child at home, He will give you the grace to do it. It won't always be easy. It won't always go smoothly. There may be times when you want to give up. You may think you are not doing a perfect job. Let me assure you that if GOD called you to the task, He will equip you for the task and you will do a far better job than whoever does it if you don't! GOD may have lessons for you in the struggle to do well and He may have a need to draw you and your child together when you admit that you don't have all the answers and have to depend on Him to direct you. He may have a lesson in submission to authority for your child.

GOD gives the grace to do the job He calls you to do.

He does not give you grace to do the job he called your child to do.

It is my prayer that whether you are working with one struggling child at home, a house full of special children, or a classroom full of "Wiggly Willies," you will find something in the pages of this book that will jumpstart you and get you going in the right direction. My husband and friends seem to think it is worth rereading a time or two, so if you get down after a few months or years, wipe off the dust and pick it up again. You may find some brand new treasures within its yellowing pages.

I welcome comments, ideas criticisms, and stories of how this book touched your life. Feel free to write. I also do some consulting by phone, but please write first giving me some background and time to pray and set up an appointment.

Joyce Herzog
The author can be contacted
C/O Simplified Learning Products
PO Box 5387
Rio Rancho, NM 87174-5387
1-800-745-8212

INDEX

25 Teaching Techniques That <u>WORK!</u>

1. I will thank God for this situation and pray for His guidance and blessing.
2. I will teach really important things first: God and the Bible.
3. I will structure routine and setting within reason.
4. I will prepare and maintain a relaxed, safe, positive atmosphere.
5. I will be consistent in demands, discipline, expectations, and attitude.
6. I will break down tasks into achievable steps
7. I will record for the student and myself short and long term goals and achievement.
8. I will keep assignments clear, attainable, and varied.
9. I will reward small achievements.
10. I will give limited choices to allow the student to have some control.
11. I will use multi-sensory presentations which involve the learner.
12. I will allow frequent physical and mental breaks.
13. I will provide frequent reviews in different learning styles.
14. I will allow for a variety of expression.
15. I will relate the unknown to previously known information.
16. I will not teach what I will have to unteach.
17. I will be as practical as possible.
18. I will give the big picture in the early stages of learning.
19. I will give the student a purpose for learning.
20. I will seek to make the information relevant and interesting.
21. I will show the student his progress at frequent intervals.
22. I will stop thinking grade level and grades and begin to think in terms of learning and progress.
23. I will concentrate on disciplining attitude more than behavior.
24. I will teach the student to cope and compensate as I attempt to train the skills he will need in life.
25. I will thank God for this situation and pray for His guidance and blessing.

A B C D E F G H I J K L M N O P Q R S T U V W X Y Z

A Accept your child with his abilities and problems.

B Believe in your child and his ability to become.

C Care about your child and his spiritual growth.

D Display your child's best work.

E Enjoy your child. This is the secret to his self-esteem.

F Figure out your child's strengths and talents.

G Give your child only the responsibilities he can handle.

H Help your child with the things he cannot do alone.

I Impress upon your child the importance of spiritual life.

J Join your child in enjoyable and meaningful activities.

K Kindle a taste for good music and literature.

L Listen to your child at two; he'll talk to you at 12.

M Model the attitudes and behavior you want to develop.

N Never belittle your child or his efforts.

O Observe your child in many situations.

P Pace your child. Help him not take on too much.

Q Question your child about what he sees, hears, and does.

R Read daily to your child from good books.

S Share your faith with your child.

T Take your child to church regularly.

U Understand that your child struggles to learn.

V Value your child's ideas.

W Worship with your child.

X eXamine your relationship with your child and with God.

Y Yield your future and that of your child to God.

Z Zero in on the eternal things!

a b c d e f g h i j k l m n o p q r s t u v w x y z

Notes...